NEW TESTAMENT MESSAGE

A Biblical-Theological Commentary

Wilfrid Harrington, O.P. and Donald Senior, C.P.

EDITORS

New Testament Message, Volume 9

ROMANS

Eugene H. Maly

Michael Glazier, Inc.
Wilmington, Delaware

MICHAEL GLAZIER, INC.
1210A King Street
Wilmington, Delaware 19806

Library of Congress Catalog Card Number: 79-55806
International Standard Book Number
  New Testament Message series: 0-89453-123-9
  ROMANS: 0-89453-132-8

Printed in the United States of America by Abbey Press

Contents

Dedicated to my family with deep love and gratitude.

Eugene H. Maly

EDITORS' PREFACE

New Testament Message is a commentary series designed to bring the best of biblical scholarship to a wide audience. Anyone who is sensitive to the mood of the church today is aware of a deep craving for the Word of God. This interest in reading and praying the scriptures is not confined to a religious elite. The desire to strengthen one's faith and to mature in prayer has brought Christians of all types and all ages to discover the beauty of the biblical message. Our age has also been heir to an avalanche of biblical scholarship. Recent archaeological finds, new manuscript evidence, and the increasing volume of specialized studies on the Bible have made possible a much more profound penetration of the biblical message. But the flood of information and its technical nature keeps much of this scholarship out of the hands of the Christian who is eager to learn but is not a specialist. *New Testament Message* is a response to this need.

The subtitle of the series is significant: "A Biblical-Theological Commentary." Each volume in the series, while drawing on up-to-date scholarship, concentrates on bringing to the fore in understandable terms the specific message of each biblical author. The essay-format (rather than a word-by-word commentary) helps the reader savor the beauty and power of the biblical message and, at the same time, understand the sensitive task of responsible biblical interpretation.

A distinctive feature of the series is the amount of space given to the "neglected" New Testament writings, such as Colossians, James, Jude, the Pastoral Letters, the Letters of Peter and John. These briefer biblical books make a significant but often overlooked contribution to the richness of the New Testament. By assigning larger than normal coverage to these books, the series hopes to give these parts of Scripture the attention they deserve.

Because *New Testament Message* is aimed at the entire English speaking world, it is a collaborative effort of international proportions. The twenty-two contributors represent biblical scholarship in North America, Ireland, Britain and Australia. Each of the contributors is a recognized expert in his or her field, has published widely, and has been chosen because of a proven ability to communicate at a popular level. And, while all of the contributors are Roman Catholic, their work is addressed to the Christian community as a whole. The New Testament is the patrimony of all Christians.It is the hope of all concerned with this series that it will bring a fuller appreciation of God's saving Word to his people.

Wilfrid Harrington, O.P.
Donald Senior, C.P.

INTRODUCTION

Background

It is the latter half of the sixth decade of the first Christian century. Paul had reached a climax in his missionary activity by the time he wrote this letter to the Roman Church. As he himself remarks in 15:19, he had "fully preached the gospel of Christ" in the greater part of the Near East, "from Jerusalem and as far round as Illyricum." He was coming to the close of this third, and, as far as we know, his last missionary journey. Probably writing from Corinth, he is looking forward to visiting the Christian community in Rome before going on to Spain (15:24,28).

Before he goes to Rome he has what he considers an urgent project to complete. For some time he had been encouraging the Gentile churches to make a contribution to the mother church in Jerusalem (1 Cor 16:1-4; 2 Cor 8-9). The purpose was not simply to alleviate the needs of the poor in that city. In Paul's mind it had the symbolic value of expressing the deep love and concern of one large segment of Christians for another smaller but more prestigious segment. Given Paul's own experience of the misunderstandings that could and did arise between Jewish and Gentile Christians, we can readily sympathize with his concern to give expression to a unity that transcends lesser differences.

Now he is ready to take the collected money to Jerusalem (Rom 15:25-32). He foresees the possibility of some misunderstanding on the part of the Jewish Christians and of open hostility on the part of the non-Christians. But he hoped that things would come out well there and that he would in good time be able to make his way to Rome for a long anticipated visit and then proceed to Spain. It is that anticipated visit that was the catalyst for the letter.

Place and Date

As already indicated, the most probable place of writing of the letter is Corinth. In Acts 20:2-3 Paul is said to have come to Greece where he spent three months. This stay was followed by a journey to Jerusalem which, in fact, was the journey whose purpose was "to bring to my nation alms and offerings" (Acts 24:17). Since he wrote the letter shortly before setting sail for his "nation" with the collection (Rom 15:25), we can conclude that he wrote it from Greece.

That it was from the city of Corinth that he wrote is suggested by several factors. It was the place where he had spent so much time preaching the gospel, and so he would have been well known there. As the largest of the Christian communities in Greece, it would have been the most likely place for a protracted stay. If chapter 16 was in some form part of the Romans letter (cf. commentary), then the reference in 16:1 to Cenchreae, Corinth's port city, would have some confirming value. Finally, on the same condition, the mention of Gaius in 16:23 as Paul's host could tally with the Gaius of Corinth whom Paul baptized at an earlier date (1 Cor 1:14).

One of the most sure dates we have for the chronology of Paul's activities is when Gallio was proconsul of Achaia (a province that included Corinth). From a Roman inscription found at Delphi in 1905 it is known that Gallio exercised his office in 51 or 52. And it was before this Gallio that Paul was brought for disobeying the law (Acts 18:12-17). Arguing from that, scholars conclude that the end of this third missionary journey (and the writing of our letter) would have occurred in late winter (Acts 20:2-6) of 57 or 58.

The Christian Church in Rome

Nothing is known of the beginnings of Christianity in Rome. The earliest probable reference to Christians being there is an account by the Roman historian, Suetonius, that Claudius, in 49 A.D., expelled all the Jews from Rome because of disturbances arising over a certain *Chresto*. The likeliest explanation is that this was a reference to Christ, suggesting that the proclaiming of Jesus as the Christ had aroused the anger of some of the Jewish citizens. Acts 18:2 mentions this decree of Claudius and indicates that some Christian Jews were among those expelled. This would mean that, after 49, the Christian community in Rome would have been almost exclusively Gentile, at least for a time.

Claudius died in 54 and doubtless a number of Jews, including some Christians, would have returned to the imperial capital. Again, granting the acceptance of c. 16 as a part of our letter, the presence of several Jewish Christians in the list of those greeted would confirm the conclusion. There are a couple of statements in the heart of the letter that would suggest the same. Thus, in 7:1 Paul says that he is "speaking to those who know the law," almost surely a reference to the Mosaic Law. Also, the manner in which Paul uses the Hebrew Scriptures in his argumentation convinces many that the readers were familiar with them. This is not, however, as strong an argument for Jewish Christians readers as it might at first seem, since the Greek version of those Scriptures was the Bible used by all the early missionaries in preaching to the Gentiles.

On the other hand, the evidence from the letter itself for Gentile Christian readers is quite strong. In 1:13-15 he speaks of his desire to come to Rome "in order that I may reap some harvest among you as well as among the rest of the Gentiles." And he goes on to speak of his obligation to Greeks, barbarians, wise and foolish, omitting any mention of Jews. Then, in 11:13 he writes, "Now I am speaking to you Gentiles." The context implies that he means what he has to say is intended for those readers who are Gentiles. At any rate, the case for a greater number of Gentile Christians in Rome seems well founded, and this may afford some insight into the letter's interpretation.

The Letter: Style and Contents

Paul was such a vivacious and even brilliant thinker that much of what he wrote has to be very carefully digested.

He gets caught up so intensely in the various questions, themselves profound enough, that the reader has to have a fairly good background to be able to follow his reasoning. It is this kind of personal involvement that makes passages like the ones on Adam's sin in 5:12-21 or on the Spirit's role in the Christian life in chapter 8 so rich, but also so difficult.

Also contributing to the difficulty is the manner in which he uses the Old Testament. The historical critical method of interpretation, which demands a careful analysis of the biblical writers' background as well as of the text itself in order to discover their meaning, was unknown in Paul's day. Rather, the Scriptures were considered the property of the community and apparently could be interpreted in a manner that the interpreter thought would best help the community. The modern reader will probably not be as convinced as Paul's original readers were by the biblical quotations.

Despite these problems, there is a richness of content in this letter to the Romans that makes it one of the most profoundly theological pieces of literature in the New Testament. This does not mean that it is an abstract, speculative study. It is a real letter written to real people concerning matters of real concern to them, even if the letter does not address problems that are unique to the Roman Church. Paul did not know the community well enough to do that. That is why his moral exhortations in 12:1 - 15:13 are probably to be taken in a general way, applicable,as Paul knew from experience, to most Christian communities.

If it had been Paul who marked off his letter in chapters and verses, as we now find it, it would have been much easier to understand how he envisioned the structure of his letter, easier, too, to interpret the emphases he was making. These divisions, however, were made from twelve to fifteen hundred years later and so represent a much later interpretation of the structure. If modern scholars were to propose a chapter and verse division of Romans, it would likely be somewhat different from the one now used. But, there would be no unanimity. Each interpreter, therefore, must attempt to justify his or her own division. The following represents this commentator's understanding of the structure of the letter. While the division was not borrowed completely from any one source, it is not presented as a uniquely creative one.

After an opening address and a statement concerning his planned visit to Rome (1:1-15), Paul summarizes the main theme on which he will elaborate, justification of both Jew and Gentile by faith (1:16-17). The inclusion of "both Jew and Gentile" should not be minimized. The relationship of the two had marked his whole missionary life and now finds its most explicit treatment. It is why his reflections on the Jews in çc. 9-11, while in one sense a departure from what he had been saying in the preceding section, are still integral to his theme.

In the letter's first major section, 1:18 - 3:20, Paul presents an almost unrelieved picture of humanity without Christ. The pagans are pictured as being without excuse for their idolatry and gross immorality (1:18-32). Then, in a general way he shows how God's wrath is visited upon all who reject him, upon "every human being who does evil, the Jew first and also the Greek" (2:1-16). This prepares the reader for the specific treatment of Jewish offenders who do not keep their own Law (2:17-29). While this might seem to question God's purpose for the Jews in the first place, Paul simply states that a sinner is a sinner and must be condemned (3:1-8). The final passage in the section (3:9-20) reaffirms the sinfulness of all.

The second major section of the letter, 3:21 - 5:21, elaborates on the theme he had announced in his opening summary statement (1:16-17), the justification of all by faith. He first makes clear that this justification does not depend on the Law, but on faith, and so cannot be the object of boasting (3:21-31). Then, in a fairly long passage (4:1-25), he shows how this kind of justification had already been anticipated in the Old Testament by God's justification of Abraham who had also believed in God, and, even before he was circumcised. God's promises to the patriarch were made before any good works were done, to show that their fulfillment does not depend on works. That is why sinners now have every reason to hope for God's glory, because God has shown his love for them by fulfilling the promise through the gift of his Son, Jesus Christ (5:1-11). The consideration of the universality of sin, complex as it is, serves to emphasize the greatness of God's gift (5:12-21).

The third major section, 6:1 - 8:39, delves more deeply into the new life that has been generated by God's gracious gift. He wants to show here also the need for walking in this new life. Baptism illustrates well what he means. Buried in the baptismal waters, Christians die with Christ so that they might eventually share in his resurrection. This "death to sin" demands a sinless life (6:1-14). Slavery also illustrates his thesis. Freed by Christ from slavery to sin, Christians become slaves to righteousness and to God (6:15-23). But this also means death to and freedom from the Law, which is replaced by the new life of the Spirit (7:1-6). Then, in a highly controverted passage (7:7-25), Paul pictures vividly the struggle within the human person for the mastery over evil, first showing the inducement to sin that laws can provide (vv. 7-12), then giving the details of the struggle itself (vv. 13-25). The eighth chapter opens up into a magnificent vision of the new age of the Spirit. He first contrasts this living in the Spirit with living in the flesh (8:1-11), and shows what is possible for children whose Father is God (vv. 12-17). The future glory of all creation is then brilliantly portrayed (vv. 18-30). A beautiful hymn to divine love concludes the whole section (vv. 31-39).

From 9:1 to 11:36 Paul, having richly described the new age of the Spirit, asks the agonizing question why his own people have apparently rejected this final stage in God's redemptive plan. He begins by noting the many privileges granted them and the nature of God's sovereign action in history (9:1-33). But Israel, to whom this good news had been proclaimed, failed to respond (10:1-21). For Paul the mystery is finally resolved in the ultimate acceptance of the gospel by the Jews after the conversion of the Gentiles (11:1-36).

The final major section of the letter, 12:1 - 15:13, is a series of ethical principles and injunctions on how to live a Christian life. The union of Christians in the Body of Christ demands a life of service to and love for one another (12:1-21). Some particular points are made on dealing with civil authority, on acting toward the neighbor, and on the Christian attitude to an age redeemed (13:1-14). The remainder of this section centers on respect for one another's consciences, especially in the matter of eating certain foods and observing certain days (14:1 - 15:13).

Paul's concluding remarks, in 15:14-33, concern his own apostolate and his plans to travel to Jerusalem with a collection for the poor and then to Rome for a visit before going on to Spain. It is questioned whether the final chapter (16:1-27) ever was part of this letter. At any rate, it contains personal greetings (vv.1-16), an expression of concern (vv.17-20), greetings from Paul's co-workers (vv.21-23), and a concluding doxology (vv.25-27).

INTRODUCTION
1:1-15

IN THIS INTRODUCTION there is contained both a greeting that includes an identification of Paul as an apostle and a succinct summary of the Christian faith (vv.1-7). He then speaks of his intention to visit the Church at Rome and to preach the gospel there (vv.8-15).

ADDRESS.
1:1-7.

> **1** Paul, a servant of Jesus Christ, called to be an apostle, set apart for the gospel of God ²which he promised beforehand through his prophets in the holy scriptures, ³the gospel concerning his Son, who was descended from David according to the flesh ⁴and designated Son of God in power according to the Spirit of holiness by his resurrection from the dead, Jesus Christ our Lord, ⁵through whom we have received grace and apostleship to bring about the obedience of faith for the sake of his name among all the nations, ⁶including yourselves who are called to belong to Jesus Christ;
>
> ⁷To all God's beloved in Rome, who are called to be saints:
>
> Grace to you and peace from God our Father and the Lord Jesus Christ.

Ancient letters always contained an address with greetings. Paul expands the form in order to identify his religious mission more clearly (v. 1) and to present the core of the Christian faith (vv. 2-6) for a church that did not know him personally. As a servant ("slave" would express Paul's mind better) of Jesus Christ, he is not ashamed to take a title abhorred by the Greeks as demeaning. But Israel's concept of a truly transcendent God, unlike the pagans', conferred greater dignity on such a God's servants (Gen 18:3; Ex 4:10; Ps 27:9). The title is, therefore, at the same time, an indication of Jesus' transcendent lordship. As an apostle, he is one sent by God (cf. Gal 1:1) with the sender's authority. His special mission ("set apart") is proclaiming the good news which God willed from the beginning.

Thus this good news is in continuity with what is found in the Hebrew Scriptures (v.2) but reaches its climax in Jesus Christ, God's Son, born of the Davidic line, and so a royal messiah. But it was his resurrection that made him able to exercise his Sonship effectively. He does this now, not "according to the flesh," but according to his own vivifying spirit as risen Lord. Paul experienced this in receiving the spiritual gift of apostleship whose goal was to have the Gentiles make that surrender to God which defines faith most radically. The Romans are among these Gentiles. God's call (*always* a prior necessity) makes them "beloved" and "saints," the latter inasmuch as they are part of God's community, the Church. To them Paul sends "grace," the wish for God's turning to them in love, and "peace," the Jewish expression for the fulness of divine blessing.

PAUL'S PLANNED VISIT.
1:8-15.

> [8]First, I thank my God through Jesus Christ for all of you, because your faith is proclaimed in all the world. [9]For God is my witness, whom I serve with my spirit in the gospel of his Son, that without ceasing I mention you

always in my prayers, [10]asking that somehow by God's will I may now at last succeed in coming to you. [11]For I long to see you, that I may impart to you some spiritual gift to strengthen you, [12]that is, that we may be mutually encouraged by each other's faith, both yours and mine. [13]I want you to know, brethren, that I have often intended to come to you (but thus far have been prevented), in order that I may reap some harvest among you as well as among the rest of the Gentiles. [14]I am under obligation both to Greeks and to barbarians, both to the wise and to the foolish: [15]so I am eager to preach the gospel to you also who are in Rome.

Paul's thanksgiving (another feature of ancient letters) for their faith is common enough (cf. 1 Thess 1:8; Phil 1:3-5; Eph 1:15-16). But the position of Rome as the seat of empire and cultural center makes the presence of a Christian faith community a source of special thanks. Paul had known of them for some time and his energetic concern for the gospel had spurred him not only to pray for them but also to plan a visit to them. The apostle has no doubt about the effectiveness of his preaching and boldly states his wish to strengthen them in their faith. But then, more delicately, he adds that it would be a mutual experience, both parties profiting from the visit. No doubt, Rome's prestige was an incentive to Paul to preach there, but we learn later that he also wanted to go on from there to Spain (15:24,28). All these concrete plans, he knows, are in God's hands (vv. 10, 13); his duty is to preach to the Greek-speaking (including the Romans) and to those of foreign tongues. Ultimately, it is the gospel that would bring him to Rome.

PAUL'S BASIC THEME

1:16-17

These two verses are generally seen by commentators as a summary statement of what Paul will be speaking about in this letter. As is clear, the emphasis is on jusficiation by faith, and this, by its nature, involves no distinction of race or social background.

> 16For I am not ashamed of the gospel: it is the power of God for salvation to every one who has faith, to the Jew first and also to the Greek. 17For in it the righteousness of God is revealed through faith for faith; as it is written, "He who through faith is righteous shall live."

Paul's confidence, even pride, in the gospel rests on his conviction that it is not mere speculative wisdom but God's active power saving believers. This salvation, understood in the fullest sense of deliverance from physical and especially spiritual evils and of promoting Christian growth, is something past, present and future. It is, therefore, a dynamic reality inaugurated in Christ's life, death and resurrection, being manifested now, and to be fully attained. It is for the believing Jew "first," both chronologically and in God's intention, but also for the "Greek"—here all Gentiles.

In this gospel power God's "righteousness" is revealed. This is another complex term in Scripture. The Greek word is also translated "justice," "justification," "uprightness."

It is God's, but always in his relationship to the world and believers. It is an action word saying what he does: ruling justly, justifying believers, making them righteous. Faith is both the means by which this revelation of righteousness is recognized and accepted and also the goal of the revelation. The prophet Habakkuk had written that the one who is loyal to God through all adversity would live, i.e., be saved from destruction by the enemy (2:4). Paul uses the saying to mean that the one who has faith in the sense indicated in v.5 will live in the full Christian way of salvation.

We see, then, that gospel, salvation, faith, righteousness are among the more significant themes presented here. They will appear throughout the rest of the epistle.

HUMANITY ALONE: SIN AND JUDGMENT
1:18 - 3:20

In this section Paul illustrates the theme just expressed by describing the human condition without Christ.

PAGAN IDOLATRY AND GOD'S WRATH.
1:18-32.

Here Paul deals with pagans; later he will take up the case of the Jewish people.

> [18]For the wrath of God is revealed from heaven against all ungodliness and wickedness of men who by their wickedness suppress the truth. [19]For what can be known about God is plain to them, because God has shown it to them. [20]Ever since the creation of the world his invisible nature, namely, his eternal power and deity, has been clearly perceived in the things that have been made. So they are without excuse; [21]for although they knew God they did not honor him as God or give thanks to him, but they became futile in their thinking and their senseless minds were darkened. [22]Claiming to be wise, they became fools, [23]and exchanged the glory of the immortal God for images resembling mortal man or birds or animals or reptiles.
>
> [24]Therefore God gave them up in the lusts of their hearts to impurity, to the dishonoring of their bodies

among themselves, ²⁵because they exchanged the truth
about God for a lie and worshiped and served the creature
rather than the Creator, who is blessed for ever! Amen.
²⁶For this reason God gave them up to dishonorable
passions. Their women exchanged natural relations for
unnatural, ²⁷and the men likewise gave up natural relations with women and were consumed with passion for
one another, men committing shameless acts with men
and receiving in their own persons the due penalty
for their error.

²⁸And since they did not see fit to acknowledge God,
God gave them up to a base mind and to improper conduct. ²⁹They were filled with all manner of wickedness,
evil, covetousness, malice. Full of envy, murder, strife,
deceit, malignity, they are gossips, ³⁰slanderers, haters
of God, insolent, haughty, boastful, inventors of evil,
disobedient to parents, ³¹foolish, faithless, heartless,
ruthless. ³²Though they know God's decree that those
who do such things deserve to die, they not only do them
but approve those who practice them.

The "for" of v.18 connects this section with the theme
just presented in the preceding verses. But it illustrates the
theme of God's righteousness by showing the opposite,
namely, the wrath of God against human depravity and
lack of faith. The word "revealed" in vv. 17 and 18 also
establishes the connection. The Greek word *orgē* can be
translated "anger" (as it is in TEV), but it is used of God so
rarely by Paul that it is considered to have a special, almost
eschatological, sense for him. "Wrath" seems to express
this better. It is presented here as the necessary divine
reaction to human perversion. But it is not to be conceived
of as a petulant or malicious spirit in God striking out at the
wicked. Rather, just as in the Scriptures punishment is
inherently associated with the concept of sin, so the "wrath
of God" is the necessary effect of unbelief. It can even be
said to express, not primarily an attitude of God, but what

happens to the sinner when God's righteousness is rejected. "God's love, resisted, is felt as wrath" (J. D. Smart). When God's wrath is contrasted with his mercy, we can say that the former "is the effect of human sin; mercy is not the effect of human goodness, but is inherent in the character of God" (C. H. Dodd).

Human wickedness is emphasized as clearly blameworthy, not due to ignorance. The "truth" the sinners suppress is that about God which, if accepted, would have led them in the opposite direction. The Greek of v.19a reads literally, "The known of God is plain to them . . ." But "the known" here means, as the context indicates, the knowable, or what can be known. That "knowable," as v.20 shows, includes those divine attributes manifested in the creation of the world. Paul is speaking here of "natural revelation," not of the self-revelation of God in history, as the Jewish people and Christians knew him. The pagans did know this about God ("know" here is taken in the sense of intellectual perception, not in the more inclusive sense of perceiving and embracing, as usual in Scriptures), but they did not act on their knowledge. To do so would have meant acknowledging him as Lord and themselves as his servants (cf. comment on v.1). For Paul, failure to do this leads necessarily to "futile" thinking and "darkened" minds. He is not condemning all the great philosophies associated with ancient Greek culture, but the religious "wisdom" they espoused. That "wisdom" is really "foolishness," manifested in the bartering away of the immortal God's glory, whereby God manifests his inner splendor to his people and thereby glorifies them, for images of created things which have no glory of themselves. Thus Paul poses a rigorous dichotomy: either the true God or empty idols. "Man must stand either under the glory of God or the nothingness of idols" (K. H. Schelkle).

The concrete effects of their failure to recognize God are presented in vv.24-31. Three times it is said that "God gave them up to"(*paredōken*; vv.24,26,28). What he "gave them up to," i.e. the vices listed in the verses that follow, is an expression of their punishment, the manifestation of God's "wrath." We can see here what we would call God's permissive will, not his absolute will, a confirmation of what was said above about God's "wrath" (v.18). First of all, they are led to all kinds of sexual deviations. This is expressed in a general way in v.24. We know how Paul looked upon the sanctity of the body from his warning to the Corinthians about fornication (1 Cor 6:15-20). Even though the pagans would not have known about the Pauline teaching concerning the body as the "temple of the Holy Spirit" (1 Cor 6:19), he still sees their sexual excesses as a dishonoring of the body. And, after that general comment, he repeats his conviction that this flowed from their rejection of the true God for the worship of or subservience to created things. The Jews of the first century were very much aware of their history and especially of the prophetic struggle against an idolatry which had led to perversion of all kinds. In this context they would have seen idolatry as the source of all wickedness, a conviction shared by Paul. This goes hand in hand with the strong monotheism of the Jewish people, which evokes from Paul the spontaneous doxology of v.25b.

In vv.26-27 the particular sexual excess of homosexuality is stressed. History records this practice among the Greeks and Paul would have been aware of it. While he would have known of the listing of "sex perversion" among the evil consequences of idolatry as attested by the book of Wisdom (14:26), a book written not much more than half a century before his time, it is not likely that that was the sole occasion of his present denunciation. It would seem that the sin itself is seen as the "due penalty" for their failure to acknowledge the true God, although the sin would have its own consequences in the person of the sinner.

Another list of vices as a consequence of their religious error is given in vv.28-31. Paul has other lists of vices similar to this (see 1 Cor 5:9-11; 2 Cor 12:20-21; Gal 5:19-21). Such lists were drawn up by the popular moralists of the day and were undoubtedly known to Paul. Thus, it does not mean that every vice listed was actually practiced by those to whom or about whom the author was writing. In this case the vices seem to be more of a social nature, with arrogant self-seeking, or covetousness, leading to all kinds of crimes against others. Paul assumes that these peole are aware of what God expects of them (cf. also 2:14-15) and that, as a result, they know the consequences of their actions, that is, death in the sense of exclusion from God's love. Their commission of these crimes in bad conscience is compounded by their approval of others doing the same thing.

We have seen that this section (vv. 18-32) was immediately preceded by what we called the basic theme of the letter, namely, the revelation of God's righteousness in the gospel. We see now how this depravity of the pagans is indeed such a revelation, but in a negative way. Paul's emphasis has been on the free rejection of that righteousness of God. It would follow that, if acceptance of the gospel leads to salvation, then its rejection must necessarily lead to perdition, a condition that manifests itself in various forms of immorality and injustice. That is why Paul could begin this section with the particle "for" (v. 18); it is the expected outcome of the theme he has announced.

GOD'S IMPARTIAL JUDGMENT.
2:1-16.

In this section Paul prepares gradually for his discussion of the Jewish people who are first explicitly mentioned in v. 17.

> **2** Therefore you have no excuse, O man, whoever you are, when you judge another; for in passing judgment upon him you condemn yourself, because you, the judge, are doing the very same things. ²We know that the judgment of God rightly falls upon those who do such things. ³Do you suppose, O man, that when you judge those who do such things and yet do them yourself, you will escape

judgment of God? ⁴Or do you presume upon the riches of his kindness and forbearance and patience? Do you not know that God's kindness is meant to lead you to repentance? ⁵But by your hard and impenitent heart you are storing up wrath for yourself on the day of wrath when God's righteous judgment will be revealed. ⁶For he will render to every man according to his works: ⁷to those who by patience in well-doing seek for glory and honor and immortality, he will give eternal life; ⁸but for those who are factious and do not obey the truth, but obey wickedness, there will be wrath and fury. ⁹There will be tribulation and distress for every human being who does evil, the Jew first and also the Greek, ¹⁰but glory and honor and peace for every one who does good, the Jew first and also the Greek. ¹¹For God shows no partiality.

¹²All who have sinned without the law will also perish without the law, and all who have sinned under the law will be judged by the law. ¹³For it is not the hearers of the law who are righteous before God, but the doers of the law who will be justified. ¹⁴When Gentiles who have not the law do by nature what the law requires, they are a law to themselves, even though they do not have the law. ¹⁵They show that what the law requires is written on their hearts, while their conscience also bears witness and their conflicting thoughts accuse or perhaps excuse them ¹⁶on that day when, according to my gospel, God judges the secrets of men by Christ Jesus.

The form of the first part of this passage (vv. 1-11) is that of the Hellenistic diatribe in which issue is taken with an imaginary opponent and supposed questions or objections are presented so they can be responded to more forcefully by the writer.

The "man" (*anthrōpos*, generic sense) of v. 1 is the supposed reader or hearer of what Paul has just written and who hypocritically (as Paul presents him) gives his full assent to all that was said: Those pagans need that kind of condemnation! But since this same person acts in the same

way (this is Paul's supposition), he is automatically condemning himself. Four forms of the word "judge" are used
in this sentence, setting the scene for the presentation of
God's judgment. That divine judgment is, in one sense, a
confirmation of the "man's" self-condemnation, because it
falls upon the one who does "such things," not on the pagan
as a pagan. Being able to issue a judgment against another
does not place one on a level that is beyond judgment of
oneself (v.3), simply because the human judge is capable of
reprehensible actions. But it is interesting how the human
nature tries to cover over one's own culpability by shifting
attention to another through judgment of that other.

The "kindness" of God in v.4 could refer to his covenant
love for his people and so allude more clearly to the Jewish
people now. But any show of divine kindness and patience is
intended ultimately to lead to reform. "History is the
school of repentance . . ." (F. J. Leenhardt). Forbearance
must not be interpreted as forgetfulness or lack of concern.
By the lack of repentance and continuation in evil the wrath
is, as it were, automatically (cf. 1:18 and comment) building
up. It will be unleashed in God's time, "the day of wrath,"
when his "just judgment" is revealed. The word emphasizes
the impartiality of God's action (cf. 2 Thess 1:5 where it
is used in the sense of an impartial *favorable* judgment).

V.6 is not a repudiation of Paul's theology of justification
by faith, but it is an important element in understanding
it. Works have a bearing on judgment. No one is ever ab-
solved from doing good; no one who does evil escapes
judgment. These two alternatives are spelled out in chiastic
form in vv.7-10: good (7), evil (8), evil (9), good (10). Doing
good for a good end results in a life ("eternal") that is
characterized by transcendence and permanence; for Paul it
will be manifested in the future (cf. 6:22). In v.8 the stress
is on the evil done, while in v.9 on the punishment meted out.
Then in v.10, to parallel v.9, the stress is on the happy end
of the workers of good. The nouns in vv. 9 and 10 are used

here, as often elsewhere, in an eschatological, or end-time, sense, just as is the "day of wrath" in v.5. In both these verses the sanction is mentioned for "the Jew first and also the Greek." The whole thrust of Paul's argument demands that we see this as a chronological priority which, in the end, does not affect the nature of the sanction. This is confirmed by v.11 which really sums up what he has been saying to his imagined partner in the diatribe.

In v.12 the word *nomos* ("law") is used for the first time in the letter, but then in this and the following three verses it, or a variant, is used eleven times. The catalyst for this frequent usage has to be the apostle's preoccupation with the situation of the Gentiles *vis-à-vis* the Jewish people who had the Mosaic Law. And this suggests that the Jewish people were in mind from the beginning of this chapter. What he says in v.12 is what he has said before, that judgment is made on the basis of actions done. The new element of law that is introduced does not change that conviction. It only means that it must be nuanced as Paul nuances it. Some are judged outside the context of the Mosaic Law, others within it. But that poses a problem, for it would seem that those who did not have this Law would be excused from obeying it.

Paul first takes up a subsidiary question (v.13), already, in fact, implicitly answered (v.6). Just hearing the Law and thus understanding it doesn't suffice. Obeying the Law is not a matter of indifference when it comes to justification. (This introduces the whole question again of justification by faith or by works, as in v.6. Paul does not take up the question, as he supposes the works of the Law here as being the fruits of the obedience of faith, not that which merits justification of itself. In other words, the contrast is between hearing and doing the Law, not between faith and the Law. But, as mentioned above, this and similar statements must be taken into consideration when discussing the Pauline doctrine on justification. If they are not, Paul could be accused of proposing a strict antinomianism, or attitude that altogether denies the significance of the works of the Law. Paul does not do this.)

In v.14 he takes up the problem of how Gentiles, who do not have the Law, could be condemned. They can do the works of the Law "by nature," or "by instinct" (NAB). There is something in them that tells them implicitly apart from the revelation granted to Israel, what is explicit in the Law. Paul would have understood this as something God-given by reason of creation; only in this sense are they "a law to themselves." But he would not have thought of it as fulfilling what Jeremiah said about the new covenant (31:33), where there is perfect conformity to God's will. From various statements of the Greek moralists he could know that they argued to right and wrong from what they felt in their hearts or from the promptings of their consciences which experienced conflicts in thoughts (v.15). The Gentile conscience will exercise its role in a special way in the end-time ("on that day"), the day of final judgment through Jesus Christ. Paul says that this is in accord with "my gospel," in the sense that for the first time in the whole discussion is the role of Jesus Christ mentioned, and he is the heart of the good news. It could also be added that the role of Christ in the final judgment is a part of Paul's gospel.

JUDGMENT ON JUDAISM.
2:17-29.

Taking up the diatribe of vv.1-11, Paul now explicitly confronts his Jewish confrere.

> [17]But if you call yourself a Jew and rely upon the law and boast of your relation to God [18]and know his will and approve what is excellent, because you are instructed in the law, [19]and if you are sure that you are a guide to the blind, a light to those who are in darkness, [20]a corrector of the foolish, a teacher of children, having in the

law the embodiment of knowledge and truth—²¹you then who teach others, will you not teach yourself? While you preach against stealing, do you steal? ²²You who say that one must not commit adultery, do you commit adultery? You who abhor idols, do you rob temples? ²³You who boast in the law, do you dishonor God by breaking the law? ²⁴For, as it is written, "The name of God is blasphemed among the Gentiles because of you."

²⁵Circumcision indeed is of value if you obey the law; but if you break the law, your circumcision becomes uncircumcision. ²⁶So, if a man who is uncircumcised keeps the precepts of the law, will not his uncircumcision be regarded as circumcision? ²⁷Then those who are physically uncircumcised but keep the law will condemn you who have the written code and circumcision but break the law. ²⁸For he is not a real Jew who is one outwardly, nor is true circumcision something external and physical. ²⁹He is a Jew who is one inwardly, and real circumcision is a matter of the heart, spiritual and not literal. His praise is not from men but from God.

When Paul mentions the many privileges of the Jewish people in this section, he implicitly supposes the many responsibilities that flow from them, responsibilities which he later shows they do not accept. Thus there is a strong ironical overcast to this listing. The Jew did consider it a privilege to be called such, and rightly so, as Paul himself would have admitted. Similarly a proper reliance on the Law and boasting of one's relation to God could be considered privileges (v.17). And each single list leads to others, such as knowing God's truth, instructing others, correcting the foolish (vv.18-20). Privilege entails responsibility which itself is a privilege. This was the conviction of the author of the Wisdom of Solomon who spoke of "the imperishable light of the law . . . to be given to the world" through the Jewish people (18:4).

But Paul never concludes the sentence he had begun in v.17. He becomes more blunt in his accusations when he

asks, rhetorically, why this privileged person does not
teach himself, why he steals, commits adultery, robs
temples. While Jewish moral standards were generally high
in comparison with the Gentiles, there is evidence in some
of the rabbinic writings of occasional laxity in these matters. Also, Paul must have been speaking from some
experience which he felt his readers would have shared.
Then in v.23 he sums up all the accusations in the one, that
of breaking the Law in which they boasted. This is the basis,
then, for his conclusion that, because of the way the Jewish
people live, the Gentiles blaspheme the name of the true
God, implying that God is the reason for the Jewish way of
acting, or that he is incapable of controlling his own people.
(The quotation is from Is 52:5 (LXX) where the reference
is to the Babylonians blaspheming Israel's God because of
his apparent inability to save them.)

With v.25 Paul appears less heated but no less denuncia-
tory. In fact, he attacks what was considered one of the
greatest privileges, or at least the greatest sign of their
privileges before God, namely, circumcision. Paul mentions
it as if it were a point made by his opponent: circumcision
is the sign of our belonging to the covenanted people and
nothing could remove that. But the apostle undercuts the
argument from the beginning by saying, in effect, that
belonging to the covenant is radically connected with the
Law (cf. Ex 19:5), and that breaking the Law annuls the
covenant. Or, as he puts it, "circumcision becomes uncircumcision." He even takes this one step further, which
would surely have outraged his supposed opponent, and
says that the (physically) uncircumcised pagan who keeps
the Law can be considered (spiritually) circumcised, which
is the manner that counts in God's sight. Thus can the pagan
"condemn"the Jew (v.27) inasmuch as this witness of spiritual
circumcision, or keeping the Law, will speak out against the
one who knew better but did not observe the Law, even
though circumcised. Paul sums up the whole question by
saying, in effect, that "a real Jew" is one whom God intended

from the beginning, one joined to him in covenant love and observing the Law from the heart. Anything external, such as circumcision, remains external unless accompanied internally by what it should signify. Jeremiah already in the OT had spoken of this circumcision of the heart (4:4), and John the Baptist had denounced the appeal to mere externals when he said that God could raise up children to Abraham from stones (Mt 3:8-9).

JEWISH OBJECTIONS.
3:1-8.

From all that Paul has said it would seem that God's self-revelation to Israel ultimately counted as nothing. Jew and pagan are alike.

> **3** Then what advantage has the Jew? Or what is the value of circumcision? ²Much in every way. To begin with, the Jews are entrusted with the oracles of God. ³What if some were unfaithful? Does their faithlessness nullify the faithfulness of God? ⁴By no means? Let God be true though every man be false, as it is written.
> "That thou mayest be justified in thy words,
> and prevail when thou art judged."
> ⁵But if our wickedness serves to show the justice of God, what shall we say? That God is unjust to inflict wrath on us? (I speak in a human way.) ⁶By no means! For then how could God judge the world? ⁷But if through my falsehood God's truthfulness abounds to his glory, why am I still being condemned as a sinner? ⁸And why not do evil that good may come?—as some people slanderously charge us with saying. Their condemnation is just.

The question in v.1 flows naturally from all that has been said. It might even be answered that it is a disadvantage to be Jewish since so much more is expected of them. But Paul could not bring himself to give that answer; his Jewish heritage is too rich. And so he begins to mention the advantages (though he never gets beyond the "first"; he mentions others in 9:4-5). They have "the oracles of God," a general expression for the Hebrew Scriptures. In saying this he uses the word *episteuthēsan* ("were entrusted"), which conjures up the notion of faith or believing (*pisteuein*). Aware that Israel's history was constantly marked by lack of faith (*epistesan*, v.3), he is distracted from his theme and goes off on another complex problem. What does this Jewish lack of faith say about the faithfulness of God who chose them? It certainly doesn't compromise it; God remains "true," or solid, dependable, faithful. And he quotes the Greek of Ps 51:6 to show that God is faithful in his "works." In fact, human lack of faith makes God's faithfulness stand out all the more clearly, even in the inflicting of his wrath on sinners because it is essential to God's faithfulness that he be a faithful and dependable judge of the world (v.6). If one were to pursue that line of argument, as Paul does, it would seem that by sinning we bring God glory. So "why not do evil that good may come?" (v.8). The argument supposes that God's glory can only be manifested in his judgment on sinners. The true believer does not need that kind of evidence to acknowledge God's glory, even though it may be confirming evidence, especially for the weak in faith. But Paul doesn't answer in that way. He simply says, rather weakly, that anyone who would accuse him of saying that one can do evil that good might come is worthy of condemnation.

UNIVERSAL SINFULNESS.
3:9-20.

This is the final preliminary statement of Paul on sinfulness before he presents the positive side.

> ⁹What then? Are we Jews any better off? No, not at all; for I have already charged that all men, both Jews

and Greeks, are under the power of sin, [10]as it is written:
"None is righteous, no, not one;
[11]no one understands, no one seeks for God.
[12]All have turned aside, together they have gone wrong;
no one does good, not even one."
[13]"Their throat is an open grave."
they use their tongues to deceive."
"The venom of asps is under their lips."
[14]"Their mouth is full of curses and bitterness."
[15]"Their feet are swift to shed blood,
[16]in their paths are ruin and misery,
[17]and the way of peace they do not know."
[18]"There is no fear of God before their eyes."
[19]Now we know that whatever the law says it speaks to those who are under the law, so that every mouth may be stopped, and the whole world may be held accountable to God. [20]For no human being will be justified in his sight by works of the law, since through the law comes knowledge of sin.

The ordinary translation of v.9 (as above) would make Paul contradict what he said in 3:1-2. But his attention is riveted here on human sinfulness itself, rather than on divine gifts, and in this sense Jews stand equally with Gentiles under God's judgment, or "under the power of sin." The Greek has literally "under sin," but the RSV translation brings out the nature of sin as a dominant force, actually personified in later passages. To dramatize this universal sinfulness, Paul quotes, somewhat freely, choice selections from Pss 14:1-3; 5:9; 140:3; 10:7; Is 59:7-8; Ps 36:1. There is evidence that the early Church had collections of such "testimonies" from the Scriptures which she used for missionary and catechetical purposes. Paul likely was using one of these. The dominant theme, of course, is alienation from God, and from v.13 on various members of the body are shown to play a part in the sinfulness. Therefore, total and universal depravity is the emphasis.

The quotations make clear that Paul uses the word "law" (*nomos,* the Torah usually, or Pentateuch) in v.19 for the Hebrew Scriptures generally. Though a rare usage (cf. 1 Cor 14:21), it is dictated by the need to impress the Jews. They might say that the quotations apply to the sinful Gentiles. Paul precludes this by saying that the Scriptures indict everyone ("every mouth," "the whole world"). He corraborates this by quoting from Ps 143:2 (Greek text), adding "by works of the law" (v.20). The law does not justify anyone; it only makes the person more aware of the sin that is forbidden (he developes this theme later in 7:7-25).

FAITH AND JUSTIFICATION
3:21 - 5:21

Paul has just indicted the human race. The "whole world" stands under God's judgment. Not even the Law given by God to Israel can justify them. But there is a solution, as he had announced in his summary statement in 1:16-17. He now proceeds to develop that statement.

ALL, JEW AND GENTILE, ARE JUSTIFIED BY FAITH. 3:21-31.

21But now the righteousness of God has been manifested apart from law, although the law and the prophets bear witness to it, 22the righteousness of God through faith in Jesus Christ for all who believe. For there is no distinction; 23since all have sinned and fall short of the glory of God, 24they are justified by his grace as a gift, through the redemption which is in Christ Jesus, 25whom God put forward as an expiation by his blood, to be received by faith. This was to show God's righteousness, because in his divine forbearance he had passed over former sins; 26it was to prove at the present time that he himself is righteous and that he justifies him who has faith in Jesus.

27Then what becomes of our boasting? It is excluded. On what principle? On the principle of works? No, but on the principle of faith. 28For we hold that a man is justified

by faith apart from works of law. ²⁹Or is God the God
of Jews only? Is he not the God of Gentiles also? Yes, of
Gentiles also, ³⁰since God is one; and he will justify the
circumcised on the ground of their faith and the uncircumcised through their faith. ³¹Do we then overthrow
the law by this faith? By no means! On the contrary,
we uphold the law.

The "but now" of v.21 both contrasts what Paul is going
to say with the situation pictured in the preceding section
and emphasizes the present realization of the good news
he shares. History has taken a new and radical turn because
of an action of God, and we as believers are in that "now"
point of time. In the sense that this "now" is so filled with
the gracious action of God in Jesus Christ some rightly call
it an "eschatological now" (the Greek word is used twelve
other times in this sense, e.g., 3:26; 5:9,11).

The divine action that constitutes this "now" is the
manifestation of God's righteousness or justice (cf. comment on 1:17). How it is manifested he will mention shortly.
In this opening verse he wants to stress again its independence of law, even though the Law (Torah or Pentateuch) and
the prophets attested to it beforehand. Once again Paul
indicates the tension he feels between the radical newness
of God's action in Christ and the continuity with the revelation of old. There was a preparation for this "radical newness," which explains the apostle's constant quotation
of the Scriptures and especially his use of the Abraham
example (c.4). In v.22 he says that the divine righteousness
is manifested "through faith in Jesus Christ for all who
believe." The latter phrase is in part a repetition of the first,
but it is added to indicate the universality of salvation,
a point necessary for those who would want to distinguish
between Jew and Gentile. Although the Greek has literally
"through faith of Jesus Christ," all commentators agree
that Christ here is the object, not the subject, of "faith,"
justifying the translation. Paul does not explain the precise

role of faith here, but it should be mentioned that, in the light of what he writes elsewhere, its role is that of *receiving* something from God by reason of its attachment to Jesus Christ.

The necessity for the universal application is simply because every human being has been estranged from God by personal sin (v.23) and so has been removed from his presence and from communion with him (God's "glory"). Because of this situation, it follows that, when they are justified, or made just or upright, it has to be by God's grace, which is something unearned, an unprovoked and spontaneous act of divine love. Paul stresses this by saying that it comes "as a gift," or "for nothing." This constant emphasis on the exclusiveness of the divine activity in justification goes hand in hand with the emphasis on the sinful condition of the human race: there is nothing that calls for justification; it has to come as pure grace. The Greek word for justification has a legal or juridical note to it. Thus God is pictured, in a sense, as a supreme Judge acquitting a prisoner. But since it is God who is declaring the person just, it would be far from Paul's mind to think that such a divine declaration would not in fact make the person just.

In the same verse another and new term is introduced, this time from the institution of slavery. Justification is through "redemption." In the Greek world this referred to the emancipation of a slave through the payment of a sum of money. But the biblical usage is not exactly parallel. Thus there is never any suggestion about the one to whom the price is paid; it is not a matter of strict bartering. Rather, biblical redemption emphasizes the action of God acquiring something for himself (Acts 20:28), buying a people for himself (1 Cor 6:20). In most cases also the note of liberation from the slavery of sin is included (Col 1:14). The perfect Old Testament parallel to this was the "redemption" of Israel from the slavery of Egypt.

Still another salvation term is introduced in v.25. God set Christ forth (on the cross?) to be an "expiation." The older translation, "propitiation," could suggest that Christ's blood placated or propitiated an angry God. This is absolutely *not* a biblical theme. In the Greek it is God who is the subject, the one who expiates, or does away with sin. Christ, especially in his crucifixion ("by his blood"), is the means of that expiation. The blood of Christ, which is an important New Testament theme, is, of course, sacrificial, but as a sign of *life* that is freely offered and of *life* that is the result. And again it is faith that receives the effects of this salvific act. The expiation of sins in Christ makes God's righteousness even more manifest by comparison with the past when God simply overlooked, or tolerated, sins in view of the great atonement that was to come in Christ.

In other words, God's righteousness or justice was not manifested by the toleration of former sins *by itself.* This toleration or "forbearance" would not have shown God's justice unless it had been directed to the "present time" when the actual destruction of sin took place by the action of Christ. And so, God's justice is really only manifested now when he justifies the one who believes in Jesus. The phrase "at the present time" (literally, "in the now time," cf. v.21 and comment) includes the special Greek word for "time" (*kairos*) which is not a mere chronological indication. Rather, it refers to a period that has been definitively marked by God's decisive action and so can be said to mark the eschatological, or end-time, age.

In this section, which is one of the more basic ones in the letter, we have seen three terms used to express what God has done in his Son, Jesus Christ. The terms are justification, redemption, and expiation. All three describe definitive and saving actions of God. All three presume a state of sin or slavery on the part of mankind. All three are, for Paul, special actions of God in the final period, even though these actions are spoken of God in the Old Testament period. All three are effected through Jesus Christ and in a special way through his sacrificial death on the cross. And the effects of all three are appropriated by human beings through faith in Jesus Christ. Of the three, justification is by far the most common in Paul's letters, indicating, as we have seen, God's free and gracious act of making just or upright those who are open to this gift through faith in Jesus Christ. Since the term does have juridical overtones, we can say that the sinner is undeservedly acquitted by God, but, as is clear from Paul's descriptions elsewhere of the effects of justification, in a sense that transcends a mere legal declaration. There is a new kind of life (cf. Gal 2:20).

The second term, redemption, is used only two other times by Paul (Rom 8:23; 1 Cor 1:30). There are two major points involved here, the moving away from a former state and the attaining of a new state. In the light of the Old Testament emphasis on God acquiring a people for himself and choosing Israel for his own inheritance or possession (Dt 7:6), it is this positive note that is probably stressed by Paul, although the note of liberation from sin is certainly included. The third term, expiation, used only here, also has an Old Testament background, associated with the so-called "mercy seat" in the Holy of Holies of the temple and with the ritual of the Day of Atonement when Israel's sins were remitted (Lev 16). Christ is the new and final "mercy seat" through whom God expiates or takes away sins. (The "mercy seat" was a golden slab on the top of the ark of the covenant. It was considered the place where God expiated the sins of his people.) What is special about all three of these terms for Paul is that they describe final climactic saving acts of God in Jesus Christ. This is why they have the aura of "realized eschatology" and why Paul can speak of the present age in such a definitive way.

In the latter part of this passage (vv.27-31) there is a greater affirmation of the effects of all this on the human person. And the first effect mentioned is the exclusion of human boasting. The word has special meaning for Paul (used eleven times, seven times in 2 Cor) both in the light of his conviction about what God has done freely and in the light of the whole question of the role of the works of the Law. Boasting, as understood here, springs from a pride in one's own self and in what one has done. But everything that he has said excludes even the possibility of such boasting. Here he states it again in more direct terms. Such boasting is excluded, he says, by reason of a basic "principle." Actually the Greek reads, "By what law? That of works? No, but by the law of faith." Paul is clearly playing here on the word "law" (*nomos*) by directly contrasting the Torah, or Law that commanded works, with the "law" of faith which presupposes no works at all and which, therefore, is not really a law. The word "principle," which the RSV uses, is thus more in accord with the meaning, but it does lose the play on words that Paul intended.

In v.28 we have a slightly different statement of the same doctrine, and also one that has played a most significant role in the controversy between Roman Catholics and the Reformers. Martin Luther had deliberately added the word "alone" after "faith," thereby adding greater emphasis to what he was convinced Paul was saying anyway. This addition was understood by Catholics to imply that Paul gave no meaning to works at all. This is clearly contrary to what he says in other places about the necessity of doing good, even in this letter (cf. 2:6,13). Apparently it was this kind of interpretation of Paul, namely, that he denied any value to good deeds, that James was struggling against in the early Church. It was why he had to assert a justification "by works and not by faith alone" (2:24; the word "alone" is part of the text here). This is what is known as antinomianism, or an against-the-law attitude. This may be what Mt 5:17-20 is striking out against also. Luther's addition, however, is understandable in the light of Paul's concern to make the works of the Law independent of justification. Thus, as one modern non-Catholic author puts it, "Man is not saved by works; but he is not saved either without works, the latter being the fruits of justification and not its cause . . ." (F. J. Leenhardt). In other words, good works must flow from justification which itself is a pure gift of God received through the openness of faith. There need be, then, no misunderstanding as long as the explanation of the wording is made clear. And the history of Christianity shows that such an explanation is always necessary.

In vv.29-30 Paul adds an interesting argument for his position from the stance of a monotheistic faith. Jews had prided themselves on their absolute monotheism which was quite consciously affirmed, especially in the great prophecies of Deutero-Isaiah against idolatry (Is 44:6-23; 46:1-13). But if there is only one God, then he must be the God of all peoples, both Jews and Gentiles. If that is true, it is difficult to think of him as having a basically different attitude toward these people with regard to their ultimate salvation. Israel was chosen from among the nations, not for its own sake, but that it might be a light "to be given to the world" (Wis 18:4). This one God, then, must will the justification, or in a broader sense, the salvation of all. If justification, then, comes through faith (which he expresses in two different ways, but without any difference in the meaning), there is no problem; Jew and Gentile are justified by the same God.

This statement leads to a question that keeps emerging. If the Gentile is justified outside or without the Law, and if the Jew is justified apart from the Law, the obvious question is: of what value is the Law? It would seem that Pauline teaching has completely devalued the Law. But the apostle would have none of that. "On the contrary," he says, "we uphold the law." Or, we give it now its true meaning and expose its proper role in the history of salvation. It prepared the way for God's act of justification by making people aware of the reality of sin (3:20; 7:7-13). But there was another way in which the Law (here understood in the broader sense of the whole Old Testament) prepared for the act of justification by faith in Christ. And the apostle addresses himself to that issue in the following chapter.

ABRAHAM JUSTIFIED BY FAITH.
4:1-25

Paul is anxious to demonstrate that he does not consider the whole of the Old Testament a harmful or even useless reality.

And, as a matter of fact we do find there the notion of faith in God as a total surrender to him that is quite similar to Paul's concept of faith, without the role played by Jesus Christ, of course. Isaiah, for example, in his confrontation with the King of Judah, demands a total trust in God before any kind of operation is undertaken (Is 7:9). The difficulty was that, along with this conviction of a basic relationship to God, there was also developed a conviction that this relationship was fundamentally affected by compliance with the written Law. At times, and especially in the later period with which Paul was well acquainted, this legalistic development tended to overshadow in importance the interior attitude of faith or trust.

In this chapter Paul shows that this faith theme was present in the Old Testament by concentrating on the case of Abraham. This was a good illustration for his purpose, since, as he notes, Abraham was justified before any of the works of the Law, especially circumcision, were imposed. The kind of argumentation used here by Paul, as elsewhere, with the frequent questions, references to Scripture, and paradoxical statements, is typical of the rabbinic method with which he would have been familiar from his earlier training (Acts 22:3).

> **4** What then shall we say about Abraham, our fore-father according to the flesh? ²For if Abraham was justified by works, he has something to boast about, but not before God. ³For what does the scripture say? "Abraham believed God, and it was reckoned to him as righteousness." ⁴Now to one who works, his wages are not reckoned as a gift but as his due. ⁵And to one who does not work but trusts him who justifies the ungodly, his faith is reckoned as righteousness. ⁶So also David pronounces a blessing upon the man to whom God reckons righteousness apart from works:
> ⁷"Blessed are those whose iniquities are forgiven, and whose sins are covered;
> ⁸blessed is the man against whom the Lord will not reckon his sin."

⁹Is this blessing pronounced only upon the circumcised, or also upon the uncircumcised? We say that faith was reckoned to Abraham as righteousness. ¹⁰How then was it reckoned to him? Was it before or after he had been circumcised? It was not after, but before he was circumcised. ¹¹He received circumcision as a sign or seal of the righteousness which he had by faith while he was still uncircumcised. The purpose was to make him the father of all who believe without being circumcised and who thus have righteousness reckoned to them, ¹²and likewise the father of the circumcised who are not merely circumcised but also follow the example of the faith which our father Abraham had before he was circumcised.

¹³The promise to Abraham and his descendants, that they should inherit the world, did not come through the law but through the righteousness of faith. ¹⁴If it is the adherents of the law who are to be the heirs, faith is null and the promise is void. ¹⁵For the law brings wrath, but where there is no law there is no transgression.

¹⁶That is why it depends on faith, in order that the promise may rest on grace and be guaranteed to all his descendants—not only to the adherents of the law but also to those who share the faith of Abraham, for he is the father of us all, ¹⁷as it is written, "I have made you the father of many nations"—in the presence of the God in whom he believed, who gives life to the dead and calls into existence the things that do not exist. ¹⁸In hope he believed against hope, that he should become the father of many nations; as he had been told, "So shall your descendants be." ¹⁹He did not weaken in faith when he considered his own body, which was as good as dead because he was about a hundred years old, or when he considered the barrenness of Sarah's womb. ²⁰No distrust made him waver concerning the promise of God, but he grew strong in his faith as he gave glory to God, ²¹fully convinced that God was able to do what he had promised. ²²That is why his faith was "reckoned to him as righteousness." ²³But the words, "it was reckoned to him," were written not for his sake alone, ²⁴but for ours also. It will

be reckoned to us who believe in him that raised from the dead Jesus our Lord, [25]who was put to death for our trespasses and raised for our justification.

In the first part of the opening verse a number of ancient manuscripts have the Greek word meaning "to find." Paul would be asking what Abraham found regarding himself in this question of justification. It would be a more direct way of approaching the problem and typical of Paul's personal emphasis. In either case the verse introduces the one who was looked upon by all Jews as the initiator of their race. This makes him all the more valuable for Paul's purpose. Abraham was not just one case of a person justified by faith. He is the one in whom all his descendants were contained and so in some way affected by what he did (this is the argument used in Heb 7:4-10).

Is there any basis for saying that Abraham was justified by works (v.2)? Many of the apostle's predecessors and contemporaries argued that there was. Abraham was said to have "kept the law of the Most High, and was taken into covenant with him; he established the covenant in his flesh, and when he was tested he was found faithful" (Sir 44:20). This early second century B.C. author seems to be referring to the patriarch's willingness to offer his son Isaac in sacrifice, as commanded by God (Gen 22:1-18). And this willingness is expressly asserted by James to be the basis for Abraham's justification by works (2:21). Paul must have been aware of these arguments from what Abraham had done, but he does not refer to them. He has a text which refers to an earlier period in the man's life. Thus he can say that if Abraham had boasted in a works-justification, it would have been only before human beings, not before God who had already justified him apart from the works. The passage he quotes is from Gen 15:6 where Abraham made his act of faith after God had told him that he would be the father of many descendants. And this faith "was reckoned to him as righteousness." Does Paul mean that, at the moment he made this act of faith, Abraham was justified? Or does he mean that the faith was a manifestation of his justification? It is difficult to believe that Paul thought the patriarch was a sinner at the time. God had already appeared to him before this and had made the promises to him (Gen 12:1-3).

In any case, the justification is a gift, not a wage for work done (v.4). In v.5 Paul talks about God justifying "the ungodly," which could suggest that he thought of Abraham as "ungodly" or "godless" at the time of his expression of faith. But would that description fit one who had been following the Lord's directives up to this time? Rather, it seems that he is simply saying that the God who does justify the ungodly reckoned or credited Abraham's faith as righteousness. The Greek word that is used for "reckon" in this chapter (eleven times) is often understood in a business context, whereby a certain amount of money is credited to one's account because of something done. Paul probably intends this meaning in order to emphasize, paradoxically, the crediting of something by God for nothing that is done.

In vv.6-8 another argument is introduced from the Old Testament. He quotes from Ps 31:1-2 which he attributes, as he does the whole Psalter, to David. While the words "justify" or "righteousness" are not used, the word "blessed" is understood by Paul to be approximate to those meanings. To be blessed is to be close to God, the source of grace. In this case the gratuity of the blessedness is brought out in the forgiveness of sins. Nothing at all is said about the sinner's good works, since they would not "count" anyway. Abraham was justified because he believed in the God of promise; this sinner is justified, or "blessed," because he believed in the God of forgiveness. The psalmist says that the Lord does "not reckon his sin." The notion of God keeping a record, or "reckoning," of one's good deeds and bad deeds is common in the history of religions. If the "good book" shows a balance in favor of the good deeds, the person is saved. Paul rules this out on the basis of this Old Testament quotation. Salvation is God's free gift to the one who believes.

With vv.9-12 a new idea is introduced in order to show Abraham's relationship to Gentile as well as to Jew. Paul asks whether the blessing mentioned in the Psalm he just quoted was intended only for the Jew (the circumcised) or also for the Gentile (the uncircumcised). The psalmist himself was undoubtedly thinking in the context of the convenanted people, therefore, of Israel. But Paul sees a deeper meaning here. The psalm says that God did not "reckon" the man's sins against him, just as the Genesis passage had said that God had "reckoned" righteousness to Abraham. The use of the same word is reason enough to argue for a similar operation taking place: God acts with the sinner in Ps 32 as he acts with Abraham in Gen 15. But with Abraham God had acted *before* the rite of circumcision was imposed (Gen 17; at least the *account* of justification by faith preceded the *account* of the circumcision, which was a sufficiently valid argument). As a matter of fact, circumcision, Paul adds, was only a "sign" or "seal" of the righteousness which the patriarch had reckoned to him while he was still uncircumcised. In Gen 17:11 it is said that circumcision was a "sign of the covenant" between God and Abraham, a point with which Paul would have been familiar (cf. Gal 3:17). But it is the justification by faith that he wants to stress here. And he sees in this chronological priority of justification a providential indication that Abraham is the father of all the uncircumcised who believe. Naturally he does not want to deny that Abraham is the father of the circumcised (the Jewish people), but they must also prove their (spiritual) descendance from him by faith. And it is this spiritual descendance which alone is of value in the final day (cf. Mt 8:11-12):

Paul next takes up the theme of inheritance in connection with Abraham (v.13). In Gen 12:2-3 God promised Abraham that he would be a great nation and that "all the families of the earth" would bless themselves by him. In Gen 13:14-17 is recorded the promise of the land and of many descendants. Repeated in various forms elsewhere (Gen 15:4,5; 17:7-8,16; 22:17-18), the promises were interpreted in Paul's time as embracing "the world" (v.13). But the major point of Paul's argument is that a divine promise made without conditions requires only faith to be fulfilled, not works. In other words, the inheritance falls to those who believe in the promise, not to those who only keep the Law. If the Law were a necessary condition, then an unconditional promise would have been useless, even false. In using the concept of inheritance, Paul depicts God as a testator, or one who makes a will. If the heirs then try to work for and so earn what they have been willed, then clearly they are showing contempt for the good will of the testator. They would rather trust their own efforts than his will. This may be in part what is behind v.15. But the law also brings wrath in the sense that, when it is broken (and it is Paul's contention that it inevitably will be), it brings down the anger of the lawmaker. Then he adds, somewhat cryptically, that "where there is no law there is no transgression." That is, there is no breaking of a (written) law. He speaks of these unhappy consequences of law more clearly elsewhere (3:20; 7:7-25).

All that Paul knows about God and his dealings with the human race through his own experience of Jesus Christ leads him to the conclusion that faith, the openness of surrender to God, is the basic requirement for salvation (v.16). Since the promise is fulfilled only in those who have faith, not in those who only keep the Law, this shows that the promise is grace, or pure gift. It is God's initiative and requires only acceptance. Also, faith as the only requirement makes it possible for those who share that faith but not the Law to inherit the promise. And that is in accord with Scripture's designation of Abraham as "the father of many nations" (Gen 17:5), that is, of all the Gentiles, as Paul understands it. In v.17b he adds a thought that somewhat disrupts the sentence structure but serves to introduce the following points. Abraham had made his act of faith in the presence of a God whose omnipotence is best illustrated in the two acts of resurrection from the dead and creation from nothing. "Faith stands always anew before death and nothingness" (K. H. Schelkle).

Abraham's faith in this kind of God engendered a hope that was contrary to all human expectations (lit., "against hope in hope he believed . . ."). The hope, of course, was that he would become the father of many nations. It was against all human expectations because both he and Sarah were far beyond the age of having children (Gen 17:17). Despite this, he did not waver in his faith, and even "grew strong" in it. In doing so he "gave glory to God." This is itself an act of faith (cf. 1:21 where unbelievers do not give glory to God). He was convinced that God could fulfill a humanly impossible promise. It should be noted that the patriarch's faith was in God, not in the promise. The promise was the object of hope. This explains why, after Isaac was born and the promise apparently fulfilled, and after Abraham was told by God to offer this only son in sacrifice, he continued to believe in God, though the hope engendered by that faith seemed shattered. It is this kind of faith that was "reckoned to him as righteousness," still another reference to Paul's favorite text, Gen 15:6.

In the last three verses of this chapter, Paul makes the application to Christians, even though he has had the Christian believer in mind all along. The "reckoning as righteousness" is said of the faith of those who believe in the Father inasmuch as he raised Jesus from the dead. This reference to the resurrection of Jesus is called for both by the earlier mention of God "who gives life to the dead" (v.17) and by the discussion of God's bringing forth life from the "good as dead" Abraham and Sarah (v.19). But again, like Abraham, Christians believe not in what God does but in the God who does it. The final verse (v.25) has been the subject of much discussion. It is such a concise, rich and profound statement of faith that it may well have been a part of the early Christian kerygma that Paul found covenient as a conclusion to his treatment of Abraham. The reference to "death for our trespasses" is almost certainly an allusion to Is 53 which describes the vicarious sacrifice of the suffering servant. It would not be proper to say that the two events mentioned here represent two distinct moments in the individual Christian's process of salvation. What is certain is that both the death and resurrection of Jesus played a positive role in the drama of salvation. This is important in view of a tendency among theologians of an earlier period to view the resurrection almost exclusively as a confirmation of Jesus' divinity or of his saving mission. As Paul makes clear in other places also (e.g., Rom 6:4), Jesus' resurrection has an influence on our lives as Christians.

Two notes should be added to the reflections on this chapter. The first concerns Paul's methodology. He uses Scripture to his advantage, ignoring passages which might distract him from his purpose. Thus in v.19 he speaks of Abraham and Sarah as beyond the age of having children, which the Genesis passage does affirm. And yet, in the preceding chapter of Genesis we are told that Abraham has a child by Hagar because of the barrenness of Sarah (16:1-4). Also, in a later chapter Abraham is said to have had six children by Keturah (25:1-2). Again, we saw in v.20 that Abraham did not waver concerning the promise of a child. But in Gen 17:17 he is said to fall to the ground and laugh when he heard the promise. But these anomalies did not disturb those used to the rabbinic method. It was the theological point that was important and a selective use of Scripture was justified in making the point.

The second note, not altogether independent of the first, concerns the modern reaction to the type of argumentation used by Paul in this chapter. It is not always a positive one because the method does not accord with our clear, logical and progressive manner of presenting a problem. But we must try to respect the Semitic mind which favors the psychological over the logical approach. A point is hammered home in a succession of ways that the mind and heart and all the emotions of the reader might be moved to accept the theological principle. And that principle, which in our case is the absolute superiority of a life of faith over a life of law, is an abiding one for all Christians and is one of which we need to be reminded over and over again.

THE HOPE OF SALVATION.
5:1-11.

Chapter 5 forms a bridge between the first part of the epistle and what follows. Having discussed the human condition without God and the act of justification by faith in Jesus Christ, Paul here sums up what he has said and then shows how that can be developed into the whole rich theology of salvation, which includes more than justification. In these first eleven verses he writes of the hope that is in us.

> **5** Therefore, since we are justified by faith, we have peace with God through our Lord Jesus Christ. ²Through him we have obtained access to this grace in which we stand, and we rejoice in our hope of sharing the glory of God. ³More than that, we rejoice in our sufferings, knowing that suffering produces endurance, ⁴and endurance produces character, and character produces hope, ⁵and hope does not disappoint us, because God's love has been poured into our hearts through the Holy Spirit which has been given to us.
> ⁶While we were still weak, at the right time Christ died for the ungodly. ⁷Why, one will hardly die for a righteous man—though perhaps for a good man one will dare even to die. ⁸But God shows his love for us in that while we were yet sinners Christ died for us. ⁹Since, therefore, we are now justified by his blood, much more shall we be saved by him from the wrath of God. ¹⁰For if

> while we were enemies we were reconciled to God by the death of his Son, much more, now that we are reconciled, shall we be saved by his life. [11]Not only so, but we also rejoice in God through our Lord Jesus Christ, through whom we have now received our reconciliation.

Alluding to all that he has said about justification by faith in Christ (the "in Christ," though not expressed here, is supposed by the relationship to the preceding verse and by the final phrase of this present verse), Paul mentions the first consequence which is "peace with God." The word "peace" is such a rich term in the Hebrew Bible, indicating the fulness of divine blessings and of the proper relationship with God. It has special meaning in the present context because he had spoken of the former state of hostility to God in the preceding chapters. That hostility and alienation are now overcome. To say that we have peace with God is to say quite briefly what he will say later in more extended form about reconciliation (vv. 10-11). All of this is possible "through our Lord Jesus Christ." Paul's Christology is so all-pervasive that he can hardly mention any salvific action or effect without referring to Christ's instrumental role.

The "grace" of v.2 is the active possession of divine friendship; it is here a kind of presence with the Lord into which we are led or introduced by Jesus. Whether a procession into the royal court is envisioned or a liturgical procession is not clear. Or it may simply be the idea of Jesus as the door to life (as in Jn 10:9). Another consequence of justification is the hope of sharing God's glory. This is closely connected with what was said in the first part of the verse and indicates that, while our access to the divine presence is a "now" reality, it does not exhaust the meaning of salvation. There is yet the fulness of God's glory, or manifestation of his loving, saving presence. That is the object of our hope in which we "rejoice." The Greek literally has "boast," a typical Pauline word which would seem to give a stronger meaning than RSV's "rejoice." Ordinarily one boasts about what one is or does on one's own. Paradoxically Paul says that we can only boast about that which is not dependent on us at all, that is, this hope which has God as its origin and its destiny.

In v.3, again, it would seem that "boast" is stronger than "rejoice." Boasting is normally exercised in relation to strength or power or something positive in ourselves. But Paul speaks of boasting in that which is normally considered evil, that is, sufferings. We boast in them not because of themselves but because they remind us of our total reliance on God (the "grace" in which we stand). It is because of that reliance that suffering can produce endurance, or the ability to continue in the right despite all odds, that endurance can produce character or the power to resist evil, and character hope. Unlike many human expectations, this hope is not illusory because it is, ultimately, the product of God's love for us. Thus, the whole salvation process, from justification to the possession of the eschatological gifts (bodily resurrection, eternal life), rests on God's love, which is as certain as the fact that he is love. The Holy Spirit's role in all this is described most succinctly here (cf. c.8). He is the channel of that love ("poured into our hearts"), the activating principle of it and witness to it. In one sense it could be said that God's love is the Holy Spirit which provides the sure foundation for Christian hope.

In an extremely forceful statement Paul shows the absolute uniqueness of God's love (vv.6-8). Human love needs some basis in objective reality, which Paul brings out so well by his apparent digression in v.7b. God's love doesn't need such a basis. God doesn't love us because we are good; rather, we are good because God loves us. The simultaneity of our lack of goodness (lit., "yet being sinners") with God's love is expressed well in v.8. A remarkable identification of motivation is present here in God's loving us and Christ's dying for us. God, therefore, is not the offended deity appeased by a self-sacrificing Christ. In fact, the close association of the work of the Holy Spirit, God and Christ in vv. 5 and 8 provides a perfectly valid "starting point for the Trinitarian dogma" (J. A. Fitzmyer).

Paul continues to work out the consequences of justification by faith in Christ (vv.9-11). In v.9 he says that "we are now justified by his blood," that is, by his passion and death. In commenting on 4:25 we noted that death and resurrection were not to be too exclusively associated with forgiveness of sins (death) and justification (resurrection). That is made clear here where death and justification are associated. But even more important is our final salvation from God's wrath (cf. comment on 1:18). Thus, Paul sets up a process here in which justification is the starting point (such a process is also at least implied in vv.1-5). In v.2 the first consequence of justification was seen as "peace." Here (v.10) it is called reconciliation to God; perhaps better, it is presented as "the inner living personal aspect" of justification (F. J. Leenhardt). At any rate, it does signify restored relationship, as does the notion of peace. But as in v.9, so here Paul speaks of the "much more" (*pollō mallon*), which is the orientation to a new life ("we shall be saved") through the risen life of Jesus. Therefore, while justification by faith is an important concept in Paul's theology, made all the more important by his conflict with the Judaizers and their emphasis on law, in the long run it must be said that the new life in Christ is for Paul "the real centre of his religion" (C. H. Dodd).

In the final verse of this passage a third reference to "boasting" ("rejoice" in RSV) is made. In the first case it was boasting in God-given hope (v.2), in the second in sufferings (v.3), and now in the ultimate and really only positive source of boasting, God himself. But unless it had been for Jesus Christ, "through whom we have now received our reconciliation," there would be no possibility of boasting. In the Scriptures reconciliation is never the movement of the human person back to God. It is, rather, God's action of drawing the person back to himself. That is why the verb is always in the passive voice (and hence the anomaly of a passive imperative in 2 Cor 5:20), or why we are said, as here, to "receive" reconciliation.

ADAM AND CHRIST.
5:12-21.

This is the final part of the long treatise (3:21-5:21) on faith and justification. The substance of his argument here is that as death reigned through the sin of Adam, so grace reigns through the saving actions of Jesus Christ.

[12]Therefore as sin came into the world through one man and death through sin, and so death spread to all men because all men sinned—[13]sin indeed was in the world before the law was given, but sin is not counted where there is no law. [14]Yet death reigned from Adam to Moses, even over those whose sins were not like the transgression of Adam, who was a type of the one who was to come.

[15]But the free gift is not like the trespass. For if many died through one man's trespass, much more have the grace of God and the free gift in the grace of that one man Jesus Christ abounded for many. [16]And the free gift is not like the effect of that one man's sin. For the judgment following one trespass brought condemnation, but the free gift following many trespasses brings justification. [17]If, because of one man's trespass, death reigned through that one man, much more will those who receive the abundance of grace and the free gift of righteousness reign in life through the one man Jesus Christ.

[18]Then as one man's trespass led to condemnation for all men, so one man's act of.righteousness leads to acquittal and life for all men. [19]For as by one man's disobedience many were made sinners, so by one man's obedience many will be made righteous. [20]Law came in, to increase the trespass; but wherein sin increased, grace abounded all the more, [21]so that, as sin reigned in death,

> grace also might reign through righteousness to eternal
> life through Jesus Christ our Lord.

The "therefore" of v.12 is typically Pauline in having, in this case, no relationship to what went before. He is in a sense clearing his mind for this final statement and the phrase is purely transitional. What he intends doing is to compare Adam's sin with Christ's saving action, and so he begins with "as" (*hōsper*, or "just as"). But he never concludes the comparison in a proper, grammatical form; he is distracted by the mention of sin and death. He begins the conclusion only in the last part of v.14.

Wisdom of Solomon 2:24 had spoken of death entering the world through the "devil's envy," which means through Adam's sin. Paul takes up this thought and says that sin (clearly intended here, not simply as the actual transgression of Adam, but as the personified force of evil) entered the world through one man. The "one man" emphasis is obvious in the context since it is compared, or better, contrasted with the "one man" Jesus Christ. This would suggest that Paul thought of Adam as an individual, although this does not affect the argument. Death, then, entered through sin. Death also is personified here and it means the termination of life, both biological and spiritual, the former being a sign of the latter. The personal transgressions of all human beings ("because all men sinned") ratified for them the death sentence.

This v.12, together with what follows, is the basis of the Catholic doctrine of original sin, even though Paul does not spell it out as clearly as did the Council of Trent. What is certain is that Paul does see the first sin as the origin in some way of all sins (cf. v.19) and that human persons are affected by the sinful condition of the world into which they are born. An important factor in Paul's thinking here is the notion of corporate personality which, in Semitic thought, means that an individual can play an *effectively* representative role with regard to others who are related to the individual in some way. The descendants of a patriarch are already contained in his loins even before their time and are in some way affected by what he does. This is even more true of Christ because of who he is; in him a new creation has appeared (2 Cor 5:17) and all are baptized into his one body (1 Cor 12:12-13). Thus, the "one man" theme is predominant here and helps to explain the doctrine of original sin (cf. 1 Cor 15:22). But Paul would agree that all human beings ratify this for themselves by personal sin (v.12d).

Paul's personification of sin and death (in the inclusive sense) becomes more intelligible if we see him envisioning these forces as ravaging the world and introducing dehumanizing conditions which perdure even after the sinner has passed on and which the personal sins of others, encouraged by these conditions, serve to enforce. The apostle's thought hangs together very well and, while sparked by his deep faith in Jesus Christ and in what he has done, reveals deep psychological insights into human nature.

Distracted by the reality of sin and death, Paul fails to complete his comparison and, instead, proceeds to expound on sin and death (vv.13-14). He associates law, which specifies what one is to do and not do, with the commission of transgressions, since once the law is known one knows when a sin is being committed (cf. also 3:20; 4:15). That is why he says that sin was "not counted," or not reckoned as being against the law, during the period between Adam and Moses. Yet during this same period, because of the sin of Adam, death "reigned." (He latches on to this word here, probably because of its forcefulness. It occurs twice again in v.17, twice in v.21, and once in 6:12, but never elsewhere in the letter.) This shows the power of the first sin which establishes Adam as a type or foreshadowing of the "last Adam." (Paul does not use the expression here, but he does in 1 Cor 15:45. This is a better expression than "second Adam," which might suggest there is another to come after Christ, as some sects hold.) The similarity between the two lies in the power of what each does, manifested in the consequences.

Those consequences are now compared. The consequence of Adam's action has already been treated (vv.12-14). That of Christ's action is called a gift, a free gift, a grace (v.15). Paul wants to stress that, while there is a correspondence between Adam and Christ, what the latter effects is much greater, far superior. (The "many" of v.15 clearly stands for "all," as v.18 makes explicit. This is a Semitic usage found also in the words of institution of the Eucharist, Mk 14:24). The differences in consequences is expressed also in the form of condemnation as against justification (v.16). And the latter comes even after many individual trespasses. The third difference is that of death and life (v.17), both of these referring primarily to relationship with God but not excluding the biological aspect. Again, Paul wants to stress the superiority of Christ's act by inserting the phrase "much more" (*pollō mallon*; so also in v.15). He continues to stress the "one man" theme.

In v.18 the differences are restated. In both cases "all men" are affected by "one man" (another pointer to "original sin"). In both cases there is a consequence, "condemnation" and "acquittal (forgiveness of sins) and life." (The NAB translation does not stress the first comparison, preferring "single offense" and "single righteous act" to "one man" as in RSV. The former is closer to the Greek text, but the latter is more in keeping with the context, Paul's emphasis on the "one man" throughout the passage.)

The strongest clearest expression of his thought is had in v.19. One man's disobedience (Adam's sin) constituted "many" (or "all"; he wants to emphasize the extent of the consequence) as sinners. While their individual personal sins ratified their sinful state, that state was present independently of them, according to this statement. On the other hand, Jesus' act of obedience will constitute "many" as righteous. The future here may refer to the fulness of salvation to be enjoyed at the end-time. This may explain why he added the word "life" to "acquittal" in v.18. While the acquittal, or justification, does mean life, the express addition of the word may suggest a fulness yet to be possessed and not fully exhausted in justification.

Law's role is not an essential one since the definitive inbreak of sin was constituted by Adam's sin. Its role, rather, was to reveal the inability of anyone or anything to save sinners, and to increase sin by showing the ways (cf. 4:20). But the increase of sin was countered by a superabundance of grace. Some note that "sin" is used in the singular here (v.20), as in v.21, and designates it, not as individual transgression, but as the personified force of evil. In that case the increase would mean the growing power of evil in the world, made possible, of course, by the individual sins. While this personified power was manifested in death, grace is manifested in eternal, that, is God-like, life. The exuberance of language in v.21b is explained by Paul's wanting to say as much as he can about the superority of Christ's act over Adam's. From v.15 on we can note his emphasis on this "much more."

THE NEW LIFE IN CHRIST
6:1 - 8:39

In these chapters Paul discusses, from various points of view, the new life that the Christian enjoys. This is a necessary part of the development of his theme because, as the experience of the Church throughout history and our own experience today can testify, when an overly charged evangelicalism expounds its doctrine of a grace-only and works-less Christianity, a form of antinomianism inevitably emerges. We need to do nothing more because we have been saved. Any sins we commit only show forth the power of God's grace in Christ. Such is the tenor of their teaching, at least by implication. Paul, very much aware of this, tackles it now. To the question whether he has been saved Paul would answer, yes, and I'm working at it.

THE NEW LIFE THROUGH BAPTISM.
6:1-14.

In this section Paul begins his discourse on the new life by showing what happens at baptism. The baptismal symbolism, being buried in and raised from the waters, is basic to all that he has here.

> **6** What shall we say then? Are we to continue in sin that grace may abound? ²By no means! How can we who died to sin still live in it? ³Do you not know that all of us who have been baptized into Christ Jesus were baptized into his death? ⁴We were buried therefore with him

by baptism into death, so that as Christ was raised from the dead by the glory of the Father, we too might walk in newness of life.

5For if we have been united with him in a death like his, we shall certainly be united with him in a resurrection like his. 6We know that our old self was crucified with him so that the sinful body might be destroyed, and we might no longer be enslaved to sin. 7For he who has died is freed from sin. 8But if we have died with Christ, we believe that we shall also live with him. 9For we know that Christ being raised from the dead will never die again; death no longer has dominion over him. 10The death he died he died to sin, once for all, but the life he lives he lives to God. 11So you also must consider yourselves dead to sin and alive to God in Christ Jesus.

12Let not sin therefore reign in your mortal bodies, to make you obey their passions. 13Do not yield your members to sin as instruments of wickedness, but yield yourselves to God as men who have been brought from death to life, and your members to God as instruments of righteousness. 14For sin will have no dominion over you, since you are not under law but under grace.

He takes up a problem that he had raised before and dismissed rather quickly on the basis of its absurdity from the point of view of God himself (3:5-8). But all this talk about the sufficiency of grace, of its superabundance, of God's mercy revealed in forgiving sins leads naturally to the question posed in v.1. Is Paul proclaiming antinomianism in all its meanings? Is he a champion of libertinism? His answer is a strenuous "no" (v.2). If we have died to sin, we no longer sin. He must now establish this death to sin. And he does it by showing how the symbolism of baptism effecting that death illustrates what it effects. The illustration is clearest in the case of baptism by immersion. There are two profound statements in v.3. The first is that we are baptized "into Christ Jesus." The preposition followed by the accusative indicates a movement into the person so that one can speak of incorporation. This is an important part of Paul's Christology and ecclesiology only elliptically expressed here. But it provides a context of realism for the remainder of what he says.

The second statement refers to baptism into Christ's death. To appreciate the significance of this it is necessary to understand the significance of Christ's death. Paul had been talking about death as a consequence of sin (c.5). But Christ's death was not that kind since he had not sinned. Rather, his death was the consequence of an act of obedience. He therefore gave a new meaning to death, one which saw it not as a consequence of sin but as the very rejection of sin, since his act of obedience to the Father's will in this total sense was by its very nature a rejection of sin. In the first Adam sin and death were inevitable companions; in the last Adam sin and death, as undergone by Jesus, are irreconcilable. That is why anyone who is baptized into this death is baptized into an act of obedience and into an act of rejection of sin.

The imagery, or symbolism, is continued in v.4. By being buried under the waters of baptism the person becomes hidden or removed from the world of the first Adam, the world of sin. There is another destiny awaiting that person and it is associated with the risen Christ. Paul says that Christ was raised from the dead but not that we are raised with him. (Only in Col 2:12; 3:1 and Eph 2:6 is this said of Christians with the use of a *syn* word, *synegeirō*, "raise with.") Probably Paul thinks this might suggest a blessed state where sin is no longer possible. And so, instead, he writes that Christ was raised that "we too *might* walk in newness of life." It should be noted that the initiative in the resurrection is the Father's who does it by his "glory" (*doxa*). God's *doxa*, like his *kabod* in the Old Testament, is the manifestation of his power in salvation history. Paul uses the expression here, not only to point up the saving character of the resurrection, but probably also to suggest the enabling power in the Christian's new way of life.

It has long been noted that there is a balance between vv. 5-7 and vv. 8-10, wherein the latter provide the explicit Christological dimension for the former, verse by verse. V. 5 seems to say that our union with Christ was achieved through our likeness to his death, which is in line with what he just said in v. 3. Here (v. 5) he uses an unusual and strong word, "grown together." Aristotle used it in the sense of being assimilated or natural, or sharing a nature. This seems to be what Paul has in mind, since he wants to emphasize the need for the Christian to be dead with Christ to sin. The union in death is a foreshadowing of a union in resurrected life. While the future tense could indicate the end-time resurrection of the Christian, the context indicates that this is at least initiated now and that the Christian should begin now walking in resurrected life.

The "old self" (v. 6) is the child of the first Adam, the one still living under the reign of sin and death. This self has been "con-crucified" (another *syn* word) that the "body of sin," that is, the human person as oriented to sin, might be done away with. Paul is thinking still of personified sin, what we would call the evil power or condition that has such control over the human race. It is the freedom from that slavery that is achieved in us through baptism. And he uses (v. 7) what was apparently a Jewish legal maxim that said that death freed one from all obligations. Similarly, the Christian, dead to the world of sin, owes nothing to that world. To continue to sin would be to deny what has happened. (In the light of the leading question in v. 1, this context of the paradox of a "Christian sinner" must always be kept in mind.)

In v. 8 Paul begins to state more explicitly the Christ-power behind the Christians' new life. A sharing in the resurrection, and therefore in the new life, flows necessarily from a sharing in Christ's death. For Paul, Christ's death and resurrection are causally, not just chronologically, related (cf. the "therefore" in Phil 2:9). The future in "we shall live with him" may refer primarily to the end-time condition but, in the context, not without reference to our present life (as in v.5 above). Christ's resurrection, in its "for us" meaning, is an open-ended saving power that continues to grow in us. The same is true of Christ's resurrection in its meaning for him, at least in the sense that his struggle with evil is over and his victory over death is won (v.9). Thus his death was historical or "once for all," and so achieved a definitive victory over sin. But his resurrection, while initiated in a historical fact (the dead body), also transcends history in that it inaugurates an on-going life "to God" (v.10). Christians, too, must consider their death to sin a definitive event and their life "to God" in the risen Christ an open-ended reality (v.11). Both these convictions contradict the objection of v.1 and bring the "doctrinal" part of this passage to a fitting close. It is probably not accidental that Paul would want his reflections to close with the phrase "in Christ Jesus," his succinct formula for expressing the intimate sharing of the Christian in the resurrected life of Christ.

In all that Paul has said in vv.1-11 there lies just under the surface a strong exhortation that is still unvoiced. How can we still live in sin? We might walk in newness of life. We might no longer be enslaved to sin. In vv.12-14 the exhortations are given full voice. While Paul has the most profound insights into what God has done in Jesus Christ, he is still a realist with regard to the human condition. That is why he says what he says in these verses. That is why he would say to the imagined one who asked him if he were saved that he was and that he was still working at it. What he had said in vv.1-11 presented the reality of the new life gained by Christians and the possibilities of its continuing growth in Christ. What he says in vv.12-14 supposes the possibility of denying the new life and re-entering the world of sin and death.

That is why he pleads with them not to let sin (again, the personified force of evil) reign as it did in the world of the first Adam. A "mortal body" is not a pejorative phrase. It refers to the human person in the present condition of this life, which means subject to temptation and to conquest by sin. But it does not mean the person as oriented to sin. In the context of grace and sin it is a neutral term. The term for "instruments," referring to "wickedness" and "righteousness" (v.13), is also a military term for weapons which Paul may well have in mind. Thus he would see the Christian life as a kind of spiritual warfare in which we are engaged (cf. 1 Thess 5:8). If the future tense of the word for "have no dominion" (v.14) is taken as a categorical prohibition, then Paul is adding another exhortation; sin *must not* have dominion (so J. Fitzmyer). If taken as a simple future as in RSV, it is a rather optimistic conclusion to this passage. Note once again here the antithetical "law" and "grace."

SLAVERY AND THE NEW LIFE.
6:15-23.

Having exploited the symbolism of baptism to indicate the new life of the Christian, Paul now makes use of the institution of slavery for the same purpose. The illustration is a forceful one and still has meaning in our day.

> [15]What then? Are we to sin because we are not under law but under grace? By no means! [16]Do you not know that if you yield yourselves to any one as obedient slaves, you are slaves of the one whom you obey, either of sin, which leads to death, or of obedience, which leads to righteousness? [17]But thanks be to God, that you who were once slaves of sin have become obedient from the heart to the standard of teaching to which you were committed, [18]and, having been set free from sin, have become slaves of righteousness. [19]I am speaking in human terms, because of your natural limitations. For just as you once yielded your members to impurity and to greater and greater iniquity, so now yield your members to righteousness for sanctification.

²⁰When you were slaves of sin, you were free in regard to righteousness. ²¹But then what return did you get from the things of which you are now ashamed? The end of those things is death.|²²But now that you have been set free from sin and have become slaves of God, the return you get is sanctification and its end, eternal life. ²³For the wages of sin is death, but the free gift of God is eternal life in Christ Jesus our Lord.

The objection introduced in v.1 is repeated in v.15. When anyone speaks of freedom from law, it is immediately inferred that the law is no longer in effect and that one can do completely as one wishes. Such an inference by some Christians seems to have plagued Paul constantly. It is a false inference precisely because, while law is no longer their master, they have a new one, Jesus Christ. In fact, law is no longer their master *because* Christ is. The concept of slavery is used here to illustrate what has happened. Slavery in the ancient world meant *total* submission of the person to the master; it was not just a paid service. Paul had already spoken of human persons as slaves (*doulos*) of Christ (cf. 1 Cor 7:22; Gal 1:10; Rom 1:1). But this submission to a transcendent Lord brought about a liberation from anything earthly, including sin and death and law. Thus, he sees slavery to sin and slavery to the Lord as irreconcilable. In v.16 he speaks of the slave "of obedience" in order to set it off from the slave "of sin," which is disobedience. But basically the Christian can be a slave only of the person, Jesus Christ.

He carries this somewhat unhappy contrast further in vv.17 and 18. In the former he says that the Romans "have become obedient . . . to the standard of teaching to which you were committed." This could almost be interpreted as a new legalism if one did not know Paul. Schelkle is probably right in saying that the apostle is emphasizing here that "faith and gospel are not feeling, disposition and experience, but the order of teaching and life of the community of the

Church." And his major thrust is, as v. 18 repeats, the change from slavery to sin to slavery to "righteousness," that is, again, to the Lord who makes righteous. In all this it must be stressed that Paul is not just saying that Christians have changed form one master (sin) to another (Christ), but that slavery to the new master automatically excludes service to the other.

He almost apologizes (v. 19) for using the imagery of slavery because he really wants to speak of Christian freedom. But the imagery is useful and can speak more forcefully to those who are still weak. So he continues to use it in speaking of their bodily members being "slavish" or "servile" (*doula*, not translated explicitly in RSV) to sin and now to righteousness. The culmination of this new slavery is "sanctification," "the process of ever-increasing consecration to the worship and service of God. Its fulness is perfect love" (V. Taylor).

The "freedom" they once enjoyed as sinners (v. 20) was, of course, a false freedom, since they were "free in regard to" (in the sense of not having) righteousness which alone can produce true freedom. Their own experience of shame because of their former sins (v. 21) attests that it was a false freedom. That kind of life leads to death (generally in the total sense with the emphasis on alienation from God). Their "freedom" as to righteousness and slavery to sin have been replaced by (true) freedom from sin and slavery to God (v. 22). While the former slavery brought no "return" (lit. "fruit," v. 21), this slavery has sanctification (cf. comment on v. 19) as its fruit, which issues forth in God-like life. The difference between the two kinds of "freedom" and the two kinds of "slavery" is strikingly pictured in v. 23. The sinner is paid like any soldier and the wages given are for work done, namely for the sins committed. And the pay is death. In contrast the justified person does not receive wages, because what is received is not earned; it is a gift. The sinner earns death; the Christian is freely given life in Christ. This is one more illustration of why the Christian should have nothing to do with sin.

DEATH TO AND FREEDOM FROM THE LAW.
7:1-6.

Several vv. in this passage constitute a bridge between what precedes and what follows (cf. E. Best). Thus death to the law (v.4) reminds one of 6:2-3, 6-7; life "in the flesh" (v.5) prepares one for 7:7-25; the "new life of the Spirit" (v.6) will be developed in 8:1-17. Despite this clear continuity, Paul does introduce a new thrust in this section. He is no longer primarily concerned with whether the Christian is free to sin, which he has effectively denied, but the Christian's relationship to law (without the article in v.1a). While some would argue that Paul is here thinking of the finely constructed Roman law, it is more likely that his primary referent is the Mosaic law. But the extension to any kind of law would not be foreign to his thought.

> 7 Do you not know, brethren—for I am speaking to those who know the law—that the law is binding on a person only during his life? ²Thus a married woman is bound by law to her husband as long as he lives; but if her husband dies she is discharged from the law concerning the husband. ³Accordingly, she will be called an adultress if she lives with another man while her husband is alive. But if her husband dies she is free from that law, and if she marries another man she is not an adulteress.
> ⁴Likewise, my brethren, you have died to the law through the body of Christ, so that you may belong to another, to him who has been raised from the dead in order that we may bear fruit for God. ⁵While we were living in the flesh, our sinful passions, aroused by the law, were at work in our members to bear fruit for death. ⁶But now we are discharged from the law, dead to that which held us captive, so that we serve not under the old written code but in the new life of the Spirit.

Paul begins by stating the obvious. Laws are not made for dead people. He could have gone on from that observation to v.4, the major point he wishes to make. But his penchant for illustrations leads him astray. In vv.2-3 he gives the example of a married woman who is bound to her husband until he dies. Then she has no more obligations with regard to him and can bind herself to another man. Presumably the woman represents the Christian, formerly bound to the law and now to Christ. But it is the husband who dies, and death is the major point that Paul wants to make, as vv. 1 and 4 show. So, from the hapless illustration we should simply draw the point, which the apostle does, that the Christian's death with Christ brings freedom from law.

In v.4 he makes this point. He speaks of this death "through the body of Christ." Is he thinking here of the individual crucified body of Jesus, as the immediate context of 6:3,6,8 would indicate? Or is he thinking of the corporate body, the Church, which the expression at times means for Paul (1 Cor 12:27; Cor 1:18, Rom 12:5)? A. Schweitzer (*The Mysticism of Paul the Apostle*, p. 188) opts for the latter in suggesting this paraphrase, "As members of the Body of Christ they have died with Christ." This would certainly be congenial to Paul's thought. But the reference to Christ's (individual) resurrection in the same verse strongly supports the primary meaning of his individual body. So, union with Christ's death brings freedom from law. He goes on to borrow another aspect from his illustration by saying that the Christian is now also free for union with "another," namely, the risen Christ. And he does this to show that it must be a (morally) productive union ("that we may bear fruit for God"), as he had already argued extensively in chapter 6. He thus exploits his figure as much as possible.

For Paul 'flesh" can mean simply this material nature (cf. 1 Cor 15:39) or human existence (2 Cor 10:3). But more often, as in v.5 and in 8:1-13, it means human nature oriented to sin. This explains why JB translates "in the flesh" as "before our conversion . . ." It is opposed to "the new life of the Spirit" (v.6). In that condition sinful passions, "aroused by the Law" (literally, "through the law," but implied is "aroused" or "occasioned"), did their works so as to (not "in order to" as in v.4) "bear fruit for death." Paul uses the same expression, "bear fruit for," as in v.4 in order to stress the contrast. But here the fruit is itself death. Since law was the occasion of sin, and, indirectly, of (spiritual) death, the Christian who had died with Christ is dead to law and hence not subject to its influence (v.6). A new kind of life has taken over, one "of the Spirit," which is contrasted with the old life "of the letter" ("the old written code" in RSV).

LAW AND SIN.
7:7-12.

In this passage, discussing the relationship between law and sin, Paul uses the first person singular, suggesting that he is speaking of his own experience. He continues this usage through the remainder of his chapter. Moreover, beginning with v.14 he uses the present tense in describing this struggle between good and evil. One of the most debated questions in the whole letter to the Romans is the identity of this "I." And the resolution of the debate can have significant implications for the interpretation of the whole passage.

There are three major candidates for the role. Paul could be referring to himself before his conversion to Christianity. Among others, Dodd argues most forcefully for this position, although he would say that Paul is presenting his own experience as typical of others before conversion. That it is autobiographical seems clear to him since other "I" passages, such as Gal 2:19-21 and Phil 3:7-14, describe his own religious experience. That it must describe his situation before conversion must be held on the basis of what he says here and elsewhere about the new life in Christ (cf. v.g. 8:1-4); in view of that how could 7:23-24 especially be said of the Christian Paul?

On the other hand, J. D. Smart argues just as forcefully that Paul is speaking of his situation as a Christian. He berates those scholars who treat the verbs of vv. 14 to 25 as though they were in the past tense instead of the present. In doing that, they mistake Paul's whole point which is to show the radical division that Christ brought into the human person, to destroy any kind of complacency that rests on salvation attained. "The peace of a complacent Christian is like the peace of a stagnant pool which Christ must destroy if new life is to grow . . ." Whether or not this is what Paul had in mind, there is no doubt that many Christians today, as through the history of the Church, could sympathize with this description and see themselves reflected in what Paul writes.

The third group of scholars, represented by Leenhardt and many modern commentators, see the "I" as a representative figure for the human person before conversion. The first hypothesis is ruled out by these scholars on the basis of complete lack of evidence that Paul had this kind of picture of himself before his conversion; on the contrary, he appears to have been a self-satisfied zealous Pharisee (Gal 1:13-14). The second hypothesis is contradicted by many statements in Paul's letters which betray, not an "obsessive self-scrutiny," but a sure awareness that, while he must yet struggle for sanctification, he is not alone: "it is no longer I who live, but Christ who lives in me" (Gal 2:20). But the representative "I" of the third hypothesis is a literary device that was known to Paul's contemporaries and becomes a powerful means of expressing the profoundly personal struggle that the sinner, all of human kind, experiences to some degree before conversion. It is this position that will be taken in the comments that follow on this and the following sections.

> [7]What then shall we say? That the law is sin? By no means! Yet, if it had not been for the law, I should not have known sin. I should not have known what it is to

covet if the law had not said, "You shall not covet." ⁸But
sin, finding opportunity in the commandment, wrought
in me all kinds of covetousness. Apart from the law sin
lies dead. ⁹I was once alive apart from the law, but when
the commandment came, sin revived and I died; ¹⁰the very
commandment which promised life proved to be death
to me. ¹¹For sin, finding opportunity in the commandments, deceived me and by it killed me. ¹²So the law is
holy, and the commandment is holy and just and good.

Paul seems constantly to be painting himself into corners
and then having to get out of them. He has already said
such apparently bad things about the law (cf. 3:20, 4:15;
5:20) that the reader could easily conclude that law and sin
are identified (v.7). He denies this in the same vehement
terms he had used in denying that it is good to sin in order
that grace might abound (6:1-2). Still, he must defend what
he really did mean to say about the law, and that is that it
brought sin-awareness. And he gives the example of the
commandment against coveting (Ex 20:17) but does not
mention a particular object as the commandment did; he
wants to suggest the coveting of anything at all. But once
the commandment is there, it is almost like telling the
person, "Look, this is something you can do, but you must
not do it." The person thus becomes aware of this tendency
and has to make a deliberate choice for God or for the
creature object of coveting. Sin, here clearly personified
as the evil force (v.8), took advantage of this inner con-
fusion and became responsible for the deed. If it hadn't
been for the law, sin would have been dead in the person.
But with the law sin comes to life and the sinner dies.
    A number of scholars see a parallel in vv.9-11 with the
temptation story of Gen 3. Paul must have had that story
in mind, but he is not doing a commentary on it. He is
dealing with the experience of everyone in history who,
it is true, must make the same kind of profound decision
that Adam and Eve did, and who, just as Eve was "beguiled"

by the serpent (Gen 3:13), is "deceived" by sin (v.11). Thus just as the serpent "used" the commandment to deceive Eve (Gen 3:1), so does sin use law to deceive everyone. And so, despite the unhappy role that law has played, it is not the evil that sin is. On the contrary, coming from God and expressing his righteousness, the law is holy and just and good.

THE INNER STRUGGLE.
7:13-25.

The struggle of the inner person here reaches its climax. Sin is pictured as so powerful a force that the individual is torn between what is known to be the right thing to do and the evil deed. Paul even seems to say that the sinner cannot avoid the evil deed. The passage is a fitting preparation for the profound treatment of Christian life in c.8.

> [13]Did that which is good, then, bring death to me? By no means! It was sin, working death in me through what is good, in order that sin might be shown to be sin, and through the commandment might become sinful beyond measure. [14]We know that the law is spiritual; but I am carnal, sold under sin. [15]I do not understand my own actions. For I do not do what I want, but I do the very thing I hate. [16]Now if I do what I do not want, I agree that the law is good. [17]So then it is no longer I that do it, but sin which dwells within me. [18]For I know that nothing good dwells within me, that is, in my flesh. I can will what is right, but I cannot do it. [19]For I do not do the good I want, but the evil I do not want is what I do. [20]Now if I do what I do not want, it is no longer I that do it, but sin which dwells within me.
>
> [21]So I find it to be a law that when I want to do right, evil lies close at hand. [22]For I delight in the law of God, in my inmost self, [23]but I see in my members another law at war with the law of my mind and making me captive to the law of sin which dwells in my members.

²⁴Wretched man that I am! Who will deliver me from
this body of death? ²⁵Thanks be to God through Jesus
Christ our Lord! So then, I of myself serve the law of God
with my mind, but with my flesh I serve the law of sin.

If the law is not sin (v.7), but something good (v.12),
did something good bring about death (v.13)? Again, Paul
makes his vigorous denial (cf. 6:1-2; 7:7). Sin and sin alone
can cause the kind of death that he is speaking of. The law
was used by sin as an occasion, and so sin used something
good to bring about death. Since the law was from God,
its violation made clear that the action was opposed to God's
will, and the true nature of sin was revealed. Since the law
is from God, it belongs to the order of God, the order of the
spirit. Despite this, it can have the effect that it does in me
because of my condition, which is "carnal," or "of the
flesh," the order of the "unspiritual" with its tendency to
sin. Paul even says that this carnal "I" is "sold under sin,"
a powerful description of the slavery of the sinner.

Slavery is a good analogy as is evident from the sinner's
actions. As the slave does what the master commands and
not what the slave desires to do, so the sinner does what sin
commands and not what the sinner would really like to do
(vv.15-16). And that the sinful actions are contrary to the
sinner's true desire proves, indirectly, the goodness of the
law. This internal struggle is so intense that the ultimate
responsibility might appear to be personified sin's rather
than the sinner's (v.17). Paul denies goodness in the person,
that is, "in the flesh," which designates the unspiritual or
the proneness to sin. It is this proneness which does not
allow the will to carry out what it sees as right, which
accounts for the paradox stated in v.19. And again in v.20
he repeats the situation of slavery expressed in v.17.

In v.21 Paul states in yet another way the inner struggle.
The word "law" (*nomos*), used twenty-three times in this
chapter alone, is here used in the sense of a general manner
of acting. In v.18b he had said, literally, "to will the good

lies close at hand to me." He now uses the same Greek verb to express the proximity of evil in the face of the will to do good. His delight really is in God's law "according to the inner man," that is, as v.23 indicates, his "mind" which must make the moral judgment. But against this proper judgment another kind of law or operating principle is at work, namely, sin. And sin wins out and procccds to dwell in the sinner. In vv.21 to 23 the word "law" is used five times and in four different senses: a general manner of acting, the torah (Paul's usual meaning), the law of sin (twice) inasmuch as sin provides the de facto principle of acting, and the law of the mind, the principle which reason suggests. These varying usages help to dramatize the intensity of the struggle. And in the use of different aspects of the human person (inmost self, members, mind) Paul is not dividing the person into various parts; each of these describes the whole person acting in different ways.

The whole passage builds up to the outburst of v.24. Understood of the sinner before conversion, as we have been understanding the "I" of this section, it is a cry of despair and of recognition of utter helplessness in the presence of this evil power within everyone. For Paul, of course, such a cry is a necessary precondition for the fruitful work of Jesus Christ in a body that is now, because of sin, under the dominion of death. While v.25a seems to be the explosive reponse to the explosive question, it is only an act of thanksgiving to God through Christ for the fact that there is a response, which will follow shortly in chapter eight. A somewhat desultory repetition of the dilemma concludes the section (v.25b).

LIFE IN THE SPIRIT.
8:1-11.

This chapter is the powerful conclusion to the section on the new life in Christ (6:1 - 8:39). Having just demonstrated, vigorously, the effect that sin has on the human person, Paul now shows what God has done for that same person through Christ and the Holy Spirit. The operative word in this chapter is "spirit" (*pneuma*), used more often than in any other chapter of the New Testament (some twenty times). Thus there is a decidedly new development here. Paul is dealing with the new age of the Spirit, and in our present section (vv.1-11) contrasts the one living in the Spirit with the one living in the flesh. We shall see, in the following sections of the chapter, that this is not fully realized salvation; there is more to come.

8 There is therefore now no condemnation for those who are in Christ Jesus. ²For the law of the Spirit of life in Christ Jesus has set me free from the law of sin and death. ³For God has done what the law, weakened by the flesh, could not do: sending his own Son in the likeness of sinful flesh and for sin, he condemned sin in the flesh, ⁴in order that the just requirement of the law might be fulfilled in us, who walk not according to the flesh but according to the Spirit. ⁵For those who live according to the flesh set their minds on the things of the flesh, but those who live according to the Spirit set their minds on the things of the Spirit. ⁶To set the mind on the flesh is death, but to set the mind on the Spirit is life and peace. ⁷For the mind that is set on the flesh is hostile to God; it does not submit to God's law, indeed it cannot; ⁸and those who are in the flesh cannot please God.

⁹But you are not in the flesh, you are in the Spirit, if in fact the Spirit of God dwells in you. Any one who does not have the Spirit of Christ does not belong to him. ¹⁰But if Christ is in you, although your bodies are dead because of sin, your spirits are alive because of righteousness. ¹¹If the Spirit of him who raised Jesus from the dead dwells in you, he who raised Christ Jesus from the dead will give life to your mortal bodies also through his Spirit which dwells in you.

A very general statement, in negative form, introduces
the section. "Condemnation" (*katakrima*), found only here
and in 5:16,18, describes the prior condition of all as a
result of Adam's sin. Leenhardt sees this chapter as a development of the statement in 7:6, while the statement in 7:5
provided the basis for the development in 7:7-25. At any rate,
what Paul says in 8:2 is quite close to what he had said in
7:6. Again, law is used in three different senses in vv. 2 and 3
(cf. comment on 7:21-23). The Spirit's law is his principle
or manner of activity. It is a divine or transcendent principle
which, as in the Old Testament (v.g., Judg 14:6), can have a
powerful effect upon a person, here a life-giving and liber-
ating effect. The liberation is from the opposing law or
principle, that of sin and death (cf. comment on 7:14-16).

In v.3 "law" is understood in its more usual Pauline
sense of the Mosaic torah. This law, though expressing
God's will and so is holy (7:12), was delivered to a sin-prone
human nature and so was "weakened," unable to achieve
its goal. God, then, took the initiative again and sent his
Son. In the light of Phil 2:6-7 especially, the Son is seen by
Paul as existing in a divine state before he was actually
"sent." Since the barrier to the law's efficacy was "sinful
flesh" (literally, "the flesh of sin"), the Son had to assume it
in order to overcome it. This is emphasized by the addition
of "and for sin" (perhaps a sacrificial reference, cf. Lev
4:22-26). Paul's use of "likeness" here is not intended to
weaken the reality of the incarnation (any more than it does
in Phil 2:7), but it does imply that the Son's human life
was not a sinful one. Because Christ lived "in the Spirit,"
he could condemn "in the flesh" anything that used flesh
as a means of warring against the Spirit, that is, sin.

V. Taylor sees in the last phrase of v.3 an indication that
Paul accepted the incarnation as part of his theology of
redemption. But considering how "in the flesh" is understood here, not just as human nature but as *sin-prone*
human nature, it is more likely a condemnation through
death and resurrection, the usual Pauline understanding
of redemption. As a result of this condemnation of sin "in
the flesh" Christians can attain a righteousness that the

law "required" but could not empower (v.4). Walking according to the Spirit, not the flesh, is a consequence of the condemnation of sin but one for which Christians are responsible; it is not a necessary consequence, but one that now at least is possible.

This contrast between flesh and Spirit is now developed. RSV's "set their minds on" is as close as possible to the Greek of v.5. Other possible translations include "their dominant outlook," "their radical interests." It is probably close to, inasmuch as it presupposes, the fundamental option of some modern moralists. That "option" or choice is either for the things of the flesh or those of the Spirit. As has been abundantly shown, the first option means death (in the total sense); the second, as just stated (v.2), means life and fulness of blessings. The flesh "mind-set" is hostile to God at least in the sense that, as Paul has shown in the preceding chapter, it cannot obey God's law and so please him.

Paul now addresses the Romans directly (vv.9-11). In these verses he speaks variously of their being in the Spirit, of the Spirit of God dwelling in them, of the Spirit of Christ belonging to them, of Christ being in them. Briefly, we can say that all these expressions mean that through the work of Jesus Christ the Spirit of God has become the operating principle in Christians, dwelling in them and enabling Christ to be in them and them to experience Christ and the Spirit. The emphasis on the Spirit keeps us in the sphere of transcendence, or the divine, and eliminates any crass local sense of the preposition "in." The emphasis on Christ reminds us that we are dealing with a real historical act of salvation, not with some purely "heavenly drama." The Roman Christians do, in fact, enjoy the activity of the Spirit (the "if" in v.9a can be translated "since") and so are not in the sin-prone condition of the flesh. One cannot belong to Christ without possessing his Spirit: the two are, since the resurrection (1:4; Acts 2:33), inseparable.

V.10 can be understood in two distinct ways. The body "dead because of sin" can refer to death with Christ in baptism (6:2-11). Then the human spirit (put in the plural in RSV in order to emphasize that meaning instead of the Holy Spirit as in vv. 9 and 11) is alive through justification. The expressions "dead through sin" and "alive through justification," however, do not seem to suggest a parallel but a contrast. The body was once dead because of sin (5:12), but the Spirit is alive in the person now because of justification. This living and life-giving Spirit, now (v.11) associated with the Father who is the ultimate principle of all saving activity, effects life not only in the present but continuously into the future, even to the resurrection of our bodies, which is seen as a kind of continuation of, or participation in, the resurrection of Jesus. To put it in other words, if the Spirit is in us, he is active in a saving way with an activity that will culminate in resurrection just as it did with Jesus.

THE SPIRIT AND GOD'S CHILDREN.
8:12-17.

In this section we have a good example of the blend of orthopraxis (right conduct) and orthodoxy (right teaching). In Paul's mind they must accompany one another. We must conquer sin in our lives (vv.12-13), and we can do so because we are God's children (vv.14-17). The ethical demands, only most generally stated here, will be treated in greater detail in chapters 12-15.

> 12So then, brethren, we are debtors, not to the flesh, to live according to the flesh—13for if you live according to the flesh you will die, but if by the Spirit you put to death the deeds of the body you will live. 14For all who are led by the Spirit of God are sons of God. 15For you did not receive the spirit of slavery to fall b ack into fear, but you have received the spirit of sonship. When we cry, "Abba! Father!" 16it is the Spirit himself bearing witness with our spirit that we are children of God, 17and if children, then heirs, heirs of God and fellow heirs with Christ, provided we suffer with him in order that we may also be glorified with him.

Paul begins by saying we are debtors, but he never gets around to saying to what or to whom. He goes on to say that we are *not* debtors to the flesh. The flesh, as sin-prone human nature, has done nothing good for us, so we need do nothing for the flesh, that is, living according to its dictates. The word "debtors" is important here and Paul clearly means that we *are* debtors to God, specifically, to the Spirit. This means that what we do, i.e., "put to death the deeds of the body," is not a gratuitous act on our part that deserves some kind of credit. The gratuitous act is what God does; we only respond to it. This is brought out in another way in v.14, where the Spirit is said to lead us, as a result of which we are God's children (cf. Gal 4:5-7). In other words, we don't file for God's paternity; the Spirit does it for us.

It is interesting, and typical of Paul, that he can say the Christian is a slave (cf. 1:1) and deny it (8:15). Of course, it is understood in different ways. Paul considers himself a slave of Jesus Christ inasmuch as he has surrendered himself totally to the Lord in faith. But he is not a slave to sin or to the flesh, which is the meaning in our passage (cf. also 6:15-20). That kind of slavery evokes fear, meaning here that servile fear that acts out of dread of punishment; it is not the fear, or sense of awe, that is found, for example, in Prov 1:7. Instead of a "spirit of slavery," Christians have received "the spirit of sonship." Paul could be thinking here of the Holy Spirit as in the whole context. This technical term for adoption (*huiothesia*, "adoption of a son") occurs only in the Pauline literature. It flows not only from the closeness of Christians to Jesus Christ, the Son of God, but also from the action of the Spirit in them, as these verses show. And one of the most significant actions in the Christian as a result of this adoption is the ability to address God by the same intimate title used by Jesus, "Abba." It is the Aramaic word of intimacy for one's father and was doubtless preserved in its original form by the early Church because it was unique to Jesus and now to Christians.

The use of the title by Christians is, paradoxically, the Spirit's way of confirming our adoption as God's children.

Thus, when we affirm God as "Father," the Spirit who
makes that possible (cf. 1 Cor 12:3) confirms what he has
already effected (cf. v.14). But being adopted children also
entails inheritance (v.17) with its ensuing special relationship
to God (the Father) and to Jesus Christ (the Son). The
notion of inheritance again implies a free gift, not an
earned one. And the inheritance is a share in God's glory
with Christ. But this must be preceded by sharing in Christ's
suffering, which was a necessary presupposition to his
own exaltation (cf. Phil 2:6-11).

THE COMING GLORY.
8:18-30.

What the Spirit has already done in us is remarkable
enough. But Paul sees a future glory that goes beyond even
this and that embraces the whole universe. This is one of
the more profound passages in the whole epistle.

> [18]I consider that the sufferings of this present time
> are not worth comparing with the glory that is to be
> revealed to us. [19]For the creation waits with eager longing
> for the revealing of the sons of God; [20]for the creation
> was subjected to futility, not of its own will but by the
> will of him who subjected it in hope; [21]because the
> creation itself will be set free from its bondage to decay
> and obtain the glorious liberty of the children of God.
> [22]We know that the whole creation has been groaning in
> travail together until now; [23]and not only the creation,
> but we ourselves, who have the first fruits of the Spirit,
> groan inwardly as we wait for adoption as sons, the
> redemption of our bodies. [24]For in this hope we were
> saved. Now hope that is seen is not hope. For who hopes
> for what he sees? [25]But if we hope for what we do not see,
> we wait for it with patience.
> [26]Likewise the Spirit helps us in our weakness; for we
> do not know how to pray as we ought, but the Spirit

himself intercedes for us with sighs too deep for words. [27]And he who searches the hearts of men knows what is the mind of the Spirit, because the Spirit intercedes for the saints according to the will of God.

[28]We know that in everything God works for good with those who love him, who are called according to his purpose. [29]For those whom he foreknew he also predestined to be conformed to the image of his Son, in order that he might be the first-born among many brethren. [30]And those whom he predestined he also called; and those whom he called he also justified; and those whom he justified he also glorified.

At the very heart of Christianity is the conviction that suffering and glory are intimately related (v.g. Mk 8:34-35; Lk 24:46; Jn 12:24; Phil 2:6-11; Col 1:24). There can be no glory without suffering. The reason for this is sin which introduced distortion and alienation and corruption into the world. These cannot be removed without the pain of a correcting reversal of the world's direction. Paul speaks of this pain and suffering here, but he wants to begin on a positive note by stressing the coming glory as of surpassing value (v.18). He says this in another way in v.19 which reads literally, "For the anxious expectation of the creation eagerly awaits the revelation of the sons of God." The sense of eager longing, twice mentioned, heightens the appreciation of the glory which creation will share with redeemed humanity. Since "creation" is here set off from "the sons of God," it is clear that Paul means the whole of material creation.

Actually it was God who, because of sin, subjected creation to its present futility or tendency to decay. But since it was not creation's doing that it experienced this subjection (v.20), God implanted in it the seed of hope. That is why all created life has this built-in urge to yearn for future glory. We find expressed here and in the following verses the solidarity of the material universe with humanity

both in the effects of sin and in the hope of glory. This
solidarity is a pervasive theme of biblical religion. Genesis
spoke of the dominion of the man and woman over "every
living thing" (1:28), of the earth being cursed because of
man's sin (3:17), of a covenant God makes with Noah and
his descendants and with "every living creature" (9:8-10).
The prophets also spoke of a renewed animal kingdom and
of a renewed earth and heavens in the end-time (Is 11:6-9;
66:22; Am 9:13). Paul also could have "reasoned" from the
resurrection of Jesus to that of all human bodies (as in v.23)
and then to the spiritual transformation of the universe.

But before creation attains this liberation (v.21), it will
necessarily experience pain issuing forth in the groaning
like that of a woman when she is about to give birth (cf.
Is 26:17). The groaning of creation is matched by the human
groaning that comes from those who already have a taste of
the glory to come inasmuch as they "have the first fruits of
the Spirit." That is, the Spirit is already with them making
them children of God (cf. v.14). But they still await that
perfect state of adoption manifested in the resurrected
and transfigured body (v.23). In this reading of the text
Paul speaks of both a realized state of adoption (v.14) and
of an eschatological or end-time state (v.23). This two-fold
form of adoption is similar to the two-fold form of salvation. In v.24 the note of "hope" is clearly directed to something not yet possessed ("who hopes for what he sees?"), that
is, eschatological salvation. Yet he can use the past tense
of the word "to save" when he writes "we were saved." The
very possibility of hoping is itself an indication that the
seed of salvation has been sown. This seed makes the hope
or expectation one that is marked by "patience" (v.25).
But that seems a weak word for what Paul is saying. There is
a sense of calm and confident endurance in the word as
used here.

To appreciate the power of the thought in vv.26-27, it is
well to note that the word for "sighs" in v.26 is the same
root word as the "groaning" in vv. 22 and 23 and can be

translated as "groanings." Some translators and commentators understand this as *"our* groanings," that is, of
Christians. But the Greek does not have "our" and the word
follows immediately after "intercedes," which is definitely
the action of the Spirit. What this means, then, is that,
while all creation groans and Christians groan, it is only
the groaning of the Spirit that makes the others effective.
The Spirit really prays for us. Paul has made similar statements before (cf. 1 Cor 12:3b; Gal 4:6; Rom 8:15-16). But
here he speaks so movingly of the native human incapacity
to address God. All we can do is "groan inwardly" (v.23)
and the Spirit makes those groans his, and God understands.
". . . now there is yet another groan of an entirely different
nature which has within itself the certainty of being heard . . .
He (the Spirit) translates man's words into the language of
the divine world" (Schelkle).

This richly worked out description of the work of the
Spirit almost demands the summary conclusion of vv.28-30.
"We know . . ." This is faith knowledge, of course, but
Paul seems to want to make a special point of what "we
know." "In everything," in health or sickness, in joy or
sorrow, in good or evil, God achieves a final good for
"those who love him." But he does not do this *because* they
love him. That would be diametrically opposed to everything Paul, and the Scriptures generally, stand for. It would
be more proper to say that they love God because he has
worked out their good (cf. Gal 4:9; 1 Jn 4:10,19; Jer 1:5).
And this, in effect, is what he does say when he adds that those
who love God were actually called by him according to *his*
(God's) purpose.

This leads him to go on to say that the calling was preceded by foreknowlege (which, as often in Scripture,
means a loving and knowing acceptance) and predestination. To understand something of this difficult concept,
we must realize that the Scriptures never conceive of God
as acting capriciously or "on the spur of the moment," nor
as acting only after he sees something in creation worthy

of his action. This would make God dependent on creation.
Therefore, if there was a good in creation God not only
had to be its ultimate cause, but also had to have intended
it from the beginning. This is the only way in which we must
understand predestination here. It is not to be thought of
as God arbitrarily choosing some individuals for salvation
and others for damnation.

What these Christians are predestined to is conformity to
Christ's image. Paul almost *had* to bring Christ into the
picture, since the last time he had referred to him was in v. 17,
and there in a passing way. But for Paul Christ is central
to his whole concept of God's saving plan and the goal of
the Christian's pilgrimage (cf. 2 Cor 3:18; 1 Cor 15:49). He
emphasizes this centrality *and* the likeness by saying that
God's whole purpose was to make Christ "the first-born
among many brethren." "First-born" means not only the
exemplar of all the others but also the principle of their
belonging to this family (cf. Col 1:18). Having made that
point, Paul continues his series of God's actions: he pre-
destines, he calls, he justifies, he glorifies. The one follows
necessarily after the other. Paul presupposes, of course,
that the Christians to whom he is writing have responded
to the call in an act of faith. The somewhat surprising
word here, at least in the form in which it is found, is
"glorify." It is in the past tense, suggesting an action
already completed. It is an anticipated eschatology, to be
sure, and founded on the awesome, saving will of God.

GOD'S LOVE, CHRISTIAN ASSURANCE.
8:31-39.

This entire section now comes to a close in this magnificent "hymn" to divine love that must impress any who
read it. Paul ends "with an impassioned testimony to the
all-sufficiency of the Love of Christ for us, a testimony
which is without parallel in the world's literature" (V.
Taylor). It is the certainty of that love that grounds all
Christian assurance.

³¹What then shall we say to this? If God is for us, who is against us? ³²He who did not spare his own Son but gave him up for us all, will he not also give us all things with him? ³³Who shall bring any charge against God's elect? It is God who justifies; ³⁴who is to condemn? Is it Christ Jesus, who died, yes, who was raised from the dead, who is at the right hand of God, who indeed intercedes for us? ³⁵Who shall separate us from the love of Christ? Shall tribulation, or distress, or persecution, or famine, or nakedness, or peril, or sword? ³⁶As it is written,

"For thy sake we are being killed all the day long;
we are regarded as sheep to be slaughtered."

³⁷No, in all these things we are more than conquerors through him who loved us. ³⁸For I am sure that neither death, nor life, nor angels, nor principalities, nor things present, nor things to come, nor powers, ³⁹nor height, nor depth, nor anything else in all creation, will be able to separate us from the love of God in Christ Jesus our Lord.

Having detailed the amazing work of God for Christians through his Son and in the Holy Spirit, Paul makes what should be an obvious conclusion: granting that God has done this, is there any obstacle to fear (v.31)? He expresses God's action in terms that evoke the emotional scene in Gen 22:2 where Abraham was told by God to "take your son, your *only* son . . . and offer him . . . as a burnt offering." God "gave him up for us all." If he did that, then there is no limit to his generosity (v.32). Still, Paul wants to spell it out by imagining some limitations. To do this he uses the symbol of the law-court (frequent in Paul and in the Bible to describe human strivings with God, v.g., Job). The questions in v.33-34 are rhetorical; their very content implies the answer. In v.34, part of a developing creed or snatches from an already existing one, Jesus is shown continuing his redeeming work in heaven, which reinforces the implied response.

In vv.35-37 other possible limitations to God's love are proposed, these based on external, natural forces. Again, the questions are rhetorical and for the same reason as above. In these cases Paul can speak from personal experience (cf. v.g., 2 Cor 11:23-33), which makes for the "impassioned" nature of his witness. He is not speculating in an ivory tower. The Psalm from which Paul quotes (44:22) had been applied by the Jewish rabbis to the martyrs in 2 Macc 7. He was probably aware of the precedent he had in making the application to Christians. The verb used in v.27 is found only here in the New Testament and literally means something like "we are super victors;" the victory far outweighs any difficulties experienced.

A third kind of possible limitations to God's love is presented in vv.38-39 and doubtless intended in an escalating sense. It is a climactic expression of the absoluteness of the bond of love between God and the Christian. "Death and life" may be an expression of polarity, like "heaven and earth," meaning everything. Angels, principalities and powers refer to supernatural beings thought by some to exercise an influence over human beings; for Paul they have no effect on God's love. "Things present" and "things to come" suggest the "chronological framework of the history of mankind" (Leenhardt), while "height" and "depth" could suggest a spatial framework. Paul has used all the explosive terms he could find to show how ineradicable is this divine force that the Scriptures know as love and which Paul has seen exhaustively demonstrated in Jesus Christ. What he has to say in chapters 12 to 15 must be read in the light of this.

THE MYSTERY OF JUDAISM
9:1 - 11:36

The depth of Paul's insight into God's love as manifested in Jesus Christ would almost necessarily have evoked a reflection on why the majority of his own people had, even if unconsciously, rejected that love. Thus, the intensity of this thought in c.8 provides a sufficient reason for this side excursion on the mystery of Judaism. (This would not exclude the possibility that Paul had had occasion to speak on this subject before in much the same terms that he uses here.)

THE SOVEREIGN ACTION OF GOD IN HISTORY.
9:1-33.

This first section sets the pace for the discussion by, first of all, noting the privileges granted to the Jewish people in their history and then affirming God's absolute sovereignty in doing what he did. We will consider this section in successive sub-sections.

> **9** I am speaking the truth in Christ, I am not lying; my conscience bears me witness in the Holy Spirit, ²that I have great sorrow and unceasing anguish in my heart. ³For I could wish that I myself were accursed and cut off from Christ for the sake of my brethren, my kinsmen by race. ⁴They are Israelites, and to them belong the sonship, the glory, the covenants, the giving of the law, the worship, and the promises; ⁵to them belong the patriarchs, and of their race, according to the flesh, is the Christ. God who is over all be blessed for ever. Amen.

Because of all that he has said about the Mosaic Law in this letter and elsewhere, it might be thought that Paul would want to have nothing to do with the Jewish people anymore. But this would be farthest from the truth, which is why he must emphasize as he does (v.1) the sorrow and anguish of his heart (v.2) because of the situation of Judiasm. So great is his concern and love for them that he could wish for exclusion from Christ's love for their good. It is clear that Paul could not mean this literally since he had just said that absolutely nothing could separate him from God's love in Christ Jesus (8:38-39). But it is a biblical way of expressing a most profound desire (cf. Ex 32:32).

The privileges of the Jews include the fact that they are Israelites, descendants of the one who was given the name of Israel by God himself (Gen 32:28) as a sign of his special role in God's plan of salvation. As part of the chosen people, they are also God's adopted sons (Ex 4:22; Hos 11:1). By "the glory" is meant a share in the divine presence manifested in special ways in Israel's history. The convenants would include those made with the patriarchs and, especially, with the people on Mt. Sinai. (If the singular is the correct reading, as some manuscripts have it, the reference would be to the Sinai Covenant). The "law" is the Mosaic *torah*, the worship the temple liturgy, and the promises those made to Abraham and others in the course of Israel's history (v.4). The patriarchs are added (v.5a) because the promises were first made to them and because, in a sense, they were to Israel what the apostles are to the Church. All of these, as Paul believed, were intended to prepare for the climactic privilege, the Messiah. And by birth, indeed, he does belong to them (v.5b). And for all these privileges Paul utters a spontaneous outburst of praise of God (v.5c). (There is good manuscript evidence for reading this praise as addressed to Christ as God. Some translations, v.g., JB, and some commentators, v.g., Schelkle, Best, Fitzmyer, adopt this reading. Paul usually reserves the term "God" for the Father. If this alternative reading is correct, the passage takes on greater theological significance.)

An ecumenical issue is raised here in the matter of translating vv. 4 and 5. The Greek reads literally, ". . . of whom the sonship and the glory and the covenants . . ." The verb is not expressed. RSV has, ". . . to them belong . . ." NAB has, "Theirs *were* the adoption, the glory, the covenants . . .," suggesting that these are no longer viable privileges. In the light of what Paul says elsewhere (v.g., 11:1-2), this latter translation can hardly be correct. Moreover, it seems most unlikely that he would bother listing privileges that he thinks have no more meaning.

> ⁶But it is not as though the word of God had failed. For not all who are descended from Israel belong to Israel, ⁷and not all are children of Abraham because they are his descendants; but "Through Isaac shall your descendants be named." ⁸This means that it is not the children of the flesh who are the children of God, but the children of the promise are reckoned as descendants. ⁹For this is what the promise said, "About this time I will return and Sarah shall have a son." ¹⁰And not only so, but also when Rebecca had conceived children by one man, our forefather Isaac, ¹¹though they were not yet born and had done nothing either good or bad, in order that God's purpose of election might continue, not because of works but because of his call, ¹²she was told, "The elder will serve the younger." ¹³As it is written, "Jacob I loved, but Esau I hated."

It would be commonly agreed by biblical scholars that one of the greatest paradoxes of biblical religion is that of absolute divine sovereignty and human freedom. Both are persistently proclaimed throughout the Scriptures. At times the latter, expressed most forecefully in rejection of God through sin, is presented in a way that appears to jeopardize God's own plan (v.g., Gen 6:1-3). At other times God's plan is pictured as though it predetermined human action, as we'll see in this section. If *human* lordship or sovereignty were involved, then a contradiction would be present. But divine lordship simply transcends by nature human comprehension and places human activity in a higher, grace-filled context. It is sufficient to note here that Paul, like the rest of Scripture, affirms both divine sovereignty and human freedom, even though our present section seems to, and does, emphasize the former.

If someone were to object that, if Paul's view of an Israel divinely chosen and apparently rejected were true, then God's "word," i.e., of promise, has failed. But Paul's reply is that, just as God's word is not to be understood in a crassly literal sense, neither is "Israel" to be understood in a strictly fleshly sense. Both are in God's sight spiritual realities (v.6). This is apparent in the case of Abraham inasmuch as the promise of a child was fulfilled not in the Ishmael born "according to the flesh," but in the Isaac born "according to the promise" (v.7; cf. Gal 4:23). Therefore, Abraham's descendants are determined primarily by God's call, just as that call made Abraham their forefather (Gen 12:1-3). That Isaac's conception was due primarily to that promise is reinforced in v.9, which must be understood in the light of Gen 18:9-15, where Sarah's laughter (v.15) can also be compared with the reaction of Paul's invisible objector.

It could be objected further that at least Isaac had been born of Sarah, the free wife, and not, like Ishmael, of a slave woman (cf. Gal 4:22). So he "merited" to be the true son. Paul counters that with the observation that both Esau and Jacob were born of the same mother and only Jacob was considered by God as the "true son" (v.10). It wasn't "flesh," it wasn't human effort (Jacob was actually chosen before birth as the one through whom the divine purpose would be fulfilled, as v.11 makes clear) that determine the divine plan. That would make God dependent on the human factor, and if he were, then why would he have needed to make a promise? (v.12). The strong statement in v.13, taken from Mal 1:2-3, illustrates the paradox mentioned above. Some see "love" and "hate" here as the equivalent of "show regard for" and "disregard." Thus God did not concern himself with the Edomites (the descendants of Esau; the discussion centers on the two nations, not on the individuals) as far as his ultimate plan is concerned. This is possible, but the Semitic penchant for terms of polarity ("heaven and earth," "life and death," "gods and men") suggests something stronger. God's hatred of Esau is a way of emphasizing his love of Jacob. It indicates a preference that has profound implications which can, ultimately, affect positively the supposed object of hatred. A good parallel is had in Lk 14:26 where the "hated" family members will, in the end, be loved in a new way, in Christ.

> [14]What shall we say then? Is there injustice on God's part? By no means! [15]For he says to Moses, "I will have mercy on whom I have mercy, and I will have compassion on whom I have compassion." [16]So it depends not upon man's will or exertion, but upon God's mercy. [17]For the scripture says to Pharaoh, "I have raised you up for the very purpose of showing my power in you, so that my name may be proclaimed in all the earth." [18]So then he has mercy upon whomever he wills, and he hardens the heart of whomever he wills.

The examples given by Paul of the success of God's plan can, understandably, raise the question of God's justice; he doesn't seem to treat everyone the same (v.14). Paul's response is to emphasize God's mercy and his non-dependence on human effort. The first is essential to his nature as he has revealed himself in "salvation history." The second is essential to his Godhead, his sovereign lordship. So, even after Israel's "original sin" in the desert (the incident of the golden calf), God has mercy (v.15; cf. Ex 33:19). Here was a clear case of God's action not depending on the human situation; in fact, Israel's sin served to confirm the divine independence and sovereignty (v.16).

But there is another side of the coin of divine sovereignty, and Paul mentions it without apparent qualms. It is the case of human evil which must also fall under the divine sovereignty in some way. And Paul admits that it does. Pharaoh is his illustration here. But first he says, in a general way, that Pharaoh, just as anyone or anything else, serves to manifest God's power and so to make his name proclaimed (v.17). Then he makes the expected statement, but one that has evoked countless studies, that God "hardens the heart of whomever he wills" (v.18).

Several points must be kept in mind. First, Paul's emphasis is on divine sovereignty, and so divine justice is not the same as human justice which depends on those for whom it is exercised. Second, the Scriptures state just as unequivocally that Pharaoh hardened his own heart (cf. Ex 7:14, 22; 8:15; 9:7). Third, Israel had a strong sense of sin as rebellion against God, as human infidelity. Fourth, Israel did not distinguish, as we do, between God's permissive will and his absolute will (cf. comments on 1:24). In the light of these established points we would have to make some kind of distinction in interpreting v.18b. That the hardening of Pharaoh's heart is an effect of God's permissive, not absolute, will is quite true. Or, it can be seen as a "sealing of a situation he (God) did not create" (Fitzmyer). Leenhardt explains, ". . . God plunges the sinner deeper into his sin when He offers His grace and it is refused." Rather, in the light of God's love of the sinner, it would be more correct to say that, faced with sin, he is moved to greater love, which, when refused, means greater sin.

> [19] You will say to me then, "Why does he still find fault? For who can resist his will?" [20] But who are you, a man, to answer back to God? Will what is molded say to its molder, "Why have you made me thus?" [21] Has the potter no right over the clay, to make out of the same lump one vessel for beauty and another for menial use? [22] What if God, desiring to show his wrath and to make known his power, has endured with much patience the vessels of wrath made for destruction, [23] in order to make known the riches of his glory for the vessels of mercy, which he has prepared beforehand for glory, [24] even us whom he has called, not

from the Jews only but also from the Gentiles? [25]As indeed he says in Hosea.

"Those who were not my people
I will call 'my people,'
and her who was not beloved
I will call 'my beloved.' "

[26]"And in the very place where it was said to them, 'You are not my people,' they will be called 'sons of the living God.' "

[27]And Isaiah cries out concerning Israel: "Though the number of the sons of Israel be as the sand of the sea, only a remnant of them will be saved; [28]for the Lord will execute his sentence upon the earth with rigor and dispatch." [29]And as Isaiah predicted, "If the Lord of hosts had not left us children, we would have fared like Sodom and been made like Gomorrah."

What we have already said can be applied to these verses, too. The questions of v.19 would be asked by rejected Israel. As often in Paul, the literary device of diatribe, which includes rhetorical questions asked by an imaginary opponent, is used. To answer these questions here he thinks, perhaps almost automatically, of a common scene in the ancient world, that of the potter molding the clay. The prophets had used that image for the same purpose that Paul does, to illustrate divine sovereignty (cf. Is 29:16; 45:9; 64:8; Jer 18:6). To our minds the absolute passivity, or better, malleability of clay makes it a poor image for the free human person. But again, Paul does recognize human freedom (8:21; Gal 5). He stresses here God's lordship and, especially, the purpose he has in mind for every creature regardless of what it turns out to be.

In v.22 there is a surface contradiction between God desiring to show his wrath and enduring "with much patience the vessels of wrath made for destruction." If God had willed absolutely to show his wrath, there would have been no need for patient endurance. We must understand, therefore, that, while God's wrath was, in the end, manifested (cf.

comments on 1:18), his patient endurance reveals what he really hoped for from Israel. On the other hand, the "vessels of mercy," including both Jews and Gentiles (v.24), both reveal God's glory and share in it (v.23). While a very general predestination is indicated here, it must be noted that he is not speaking of individual predestination to salvation or damnation.

In vv.25-29 Paul uses a series of quotations from Hosea and Isaiah to illustrate the call of the Gentiles and the salvation of a remnant of Israel (cf. the comment on "testimonies" in 3:10). The first quotation, from Ho 2:23, refers to God's taking back fallen Israel. But Paul applies it to the Gentiles. This is not a strange choice of a text, however, as Dodd argues, because Israel's infidelity had in fact made her like the pagan nations (as Amos openly states in 9:7). Moreover, the "not my people" phrase would have been almost automatically recalled when thinking of Gentiles. The second text, from Ho 1:10, confirms the creative action of God with regard to the Gentiles.

The Isaian quotations in vv.27-29 are taken from 10:22-23 and 1:10 and stress the "remnant" theme. "Remnant" can be understood in a negative way in the sense that destruction will be so great that only a few will remain. Or it can be understood in a positive way in the sense that, despite the great destruction, there will be a seed for hope. That Paul is thinking principally in the latter sense would seem to be indicated by the general context of this whole section where he is concerned to show that God's word had not failed (9:6).

> [30]What shall we say, then? That Gentiles who did not pursue righteousness have attained it, that is, righteousness through faith; [31]but that Israel who pursued the righteousness which is based on law did not succeed in fulfilling that law. [32]Why? Because they did not pursue it through faith, but as if it were based on works. They have stumbled over the stumbling stone, [33]as it is written, "Behold, I am laying in Zion a stone that will make men stumble, a rock that will make them fall; and he who believes in him will not be put to shame."

This final passage in the chapter follows well enough on the preceding but also prepares for the next chapter with its emphasis on "a disobedient and contrary people" (10:21). Having stated that the Gentiles have attained salvation while only a remnant of the Jews have, Paul explains the paradox, not now on the basis of testimonies from Scripture, but on the basis of his doctrine of justification by faith (3:21-5:21). For Paul to "pursue righteousness" suggests human effort which he sees the Jews as having done with their emphasis on keeping the law. He cannot accept this kind of "works righteousness" (vv.31-32). Faith is not the result of human effort but is a gift from God which the Gentiles accepted.

This conjures up in Paul's mind the image of a stone of stumbling (cf. Is 8:14), since it is clear to him that Israel has "stumbled" in some way (v.32b). It is likely that in the early Christian tradition Christ was looked upon as the cornerstone of a new building rejected by some (cf. Mk 12:10-11). Paul takes this up and sees Christ as the stumbling stone mentioned in Isaiah (his "quote" is an artificial combining of Is 28:16 and 8:14, typical of early exegesis). The Gentile world, of course, is the one that "believes in him" (v.33). This prepares his readers for a further examination of Israel's "stumbling."

THE HUMAN (ISRAEL'S) RESPONSIBILITY. 10:1-21.

Having shown the sovereign action of God in history very forcefully (so forcefully, in fact, that the treatment needed some subtle interpretation at times), Paul now argues the human side of the coin, Israel's responsibility with regard to faith. After a brief expression of his personal concern for Israel (vv.1-2), he first shows that the "way of faith" is accessible to all and not difficult at all (vv.3-13). He then shows that, while the world must be proclaimed in order to be believed, Israel has had the opportunity to hear the word, but she failed to respond (vv.14-21).

10   Brethren, my heart's desire and prayer to God for them is that they may be saved. ²I bear them witness that they have a zeal for God, but it is not enlightened. ³For, being ignorant of the righteousness that comes from God, and seeking to establish their own, they did not submit to God's righteousness. ⁴For Christ is the end of the law, that every one who has faith may be justified.

⁵Moses writes that the man who practices the righteousness which is based on the law shall live by it. ⁶But the righteousness based on faith says, Do not say in your heart, "Who will ascend into heaven?" (that is, to bring Christ down) ⁷or "Who will descend into the abyss?" (that is, to bring Christ up from the dead). ⁸But what does it say? The word is near you, on your lips and in your heart (that is, the word of faith which we preach); ⁹because, if you confess with your lips that Jesus is Lord and believe in your heart that God raised him from the dead, you will be saved. ¹⁰For man believes with his heart and so is justified, and he confesses with his lips and so is saved. ¹¹The scripture says, "No one who believes in him will be put to shame." ¹²For there is no distinction between Jew and Greek; the same Lord is Lord of all and bestows his riches upon all who call upon him. ¹³For, "every one who calls upon the name of the Lord will be saved."

Despite all that he has said and will say about Israel's fall and her responsibility for it, Paul repeats (cf. 9:1-3) his expression of personal concern, here in the form of his own desire and prayer for her salvation. Clearly he does not see her condition as hopeless (v.1). Paul, perhaps best of all, could vouch for her zeal, but it was not in accord with a proper understanding of God's will as known through the Scriptures (v.2). They did not recognize God's righteousness but wanted to create their own through their efforts in keeping the law (v.3). In the case of God's righteousness (and Paul may be thinking, in this second usage, of Christ as the manifestation of God's righteousness, which would give clearer meaning to the "for" of v.4) all that is necessary is the act of submission which is faith. For Paul, of course, Christ is the object of this faith and, since he is the medium of a totally new creation (cf. 2 Cor 5:17), he must mean law's end (v.4). (Matthew sees him as the end in the sense of fulfillment of the law, giving it a meaning it was never thought it could have; cf. 5:17-20).

The statement in v.5 about righteousness based on the law can be understood in several ways. Paul is referring here to Lev 18:5. Most commentators say that Paul is taking the statement seriously and is suggesting, as in Gal 3:12 where he uses the same passage, that trying to live by the law proves that it is impossible to do so. So, while the statement may be true in itself, human history shows that it has not in fact been verified; all are sinners despite, or even because of, the law (5:12-13, 20). A faith-righteousness, on the other hand, does not make impossible demands. In Deuteronomy 30:11-13, Moses is said to claim that the law is not "up in the sky" or "across the sea," that is, inaccessible. Paul takes off from that passage and adapts it to Christ's incarnation and resurrection (vv.6-7). He is saying that faith does not have to bring about these transcendent events. God effects them; faith accepts them as saving events. (There may also be an allusion here to Ps 107:26). He introduced this reference with, "Do not say in your heart . . ." This comes from Dt 9:4 where the author is warning the people that they should not claim they attained the promised land by their own righteousness. The Deuteronomist had a much clearer perception of the necessary priority of the divine action for Israel's salvation (cf. Dt 7:7-8) and so was much closer to Paul's thinking than was the author of Leviticus. That is why Paul quotes him again in v.8 (cf. Dt 30:14). The Deuteronomist was, of course, thinking of the "word" of the law which he saw as "not too hard" or "far off" or up in "heaven" or "beyond the sea" (30:11-13); it was instead a "near word," one that was "on your lips and in your heart." Paul accepts all of this except that for him the "word" is the Christian message which only needs acceptance in faith.

The "lips" and "heart" play a necessary role in the Christian's life inasmuch as the faith-surrender that comes from
the heart has to be accompanied by the actual confession,
whenever that is called for, that Jesus is Lord (v.9). Paul
associates this confession of lordship with belief in the resurrection which was the catalyst for the confession (1:4). The
lordship of Jesus, seen as parallel with that of God in the
Old Testament, is central to Christianity and was one of the
oldest creedal formulas. Paul has elaborated on the name
"Lord" in Phil 2:6-11. In v.10 he associates belief with justification and confession with salvation. Leenhardt notes that
this must be eschatological salvation granted the one who
is not ashamed to confess the Lord in a lifetime of persecution or adversity. That is a beautiful insight, although it may
be going beyond what Paul had in mind. In confirmation of
his remarks about faith he uses an Isaian quote (28:16),
changing it slightly to stress the universality (v.11).

The acceptance of Jesus as Lord instead of reliance on the
law breaks down any distinction between Jew and Gentile
as far as salvation is concerned (v.12). Jesus is Lord for all.
And just as the title "Lord" was transferred to him from the
Father, so is the characteristic of bestowing his riches on
those who confess him (cf. 2:4, 9:23, 11:33, where this is said
of God). In the same spirit Paul takes a quotation from Joel
(2:32), which was originally applied to Yahweh, and applies
it to the risen Christ (v.13).

> [14]But how are men to call upon him in whom they have
> not believed? And how are they to believe in him of whom
> they have never heard? And how are they to hear without
> a preacher? [15]And how can men preach unless they are
> sent? As it is written, "How beautiful are the feet of those
> who preach good news!" [16]But they have not all obeyed
> the gospel: for Isaiah says, "Lord, who has believed what
> he has heard from us?" [17]So faith comes from what is
> heard, and what is heard comes by the preaching of
> Christ.

¹⁸But I ask, have they not heard? Indeed they have; for "Their voice has gone out to all the earth, and their words to the ends of the world." ¹⁹Again I ask, did Israel not understand? First Moses says, "I will make you jealous of those who are not a nation; with a foolish nation I will make you angry." ²⁰Then Isaiah is so bold as to say, "I have been found by those who did not seek me; I have shown myself to those who did not ask for me." ²¹But of Israel he says, "All day long I have held out my hands to a disobedient and contrary people."

Having established faith-righteousness as something available to all who accept Jesus as Lord, Paul now makes a pointed application to Israel. He does this, first of all, by listing the prerequirements, that is, the factors that must be realized before one can say, "I believe." These may seem rather obvious to us, but each step mentioned here had great significance for the Semitic mind. The first question (v. 14a) takes up from the preceding verse and is really the final question: is it that they have not believed? And Paul will have to answer at the end of the argument (v. 21) that they have not. But he wants to show first that the other steps have been realized. Hearing the message is the most immediate prerequirement to faith. That was the way in which radical conversion was effected in the biblical world. The prophets were constantly reminding the people to "hear the word of the Lord" (v.g., Is 28:14; Jer 2:4; Ezek 6:3). This is also a frequent charge of the Deuteronomist (v.g., 6:3,4; 9:1) whom Paul has already quoted a couple of times in this section (10:6-8).

Hearing, of course, presumes a herald, an official proclaimer of the good news. It is not just anyone who can bring the message. The preacher must be duly authorized if there is to be credibility (v.15). And authorization means that the preacher is sent (the verb *apostellein*, "to send," is used, suggesting perhaps the apostolic office). The beautiful passage

from Isaiah (52:7) would be more appropriate after the preceding verse about the preacher. But Paul may have wanted
to complete his list of prerequisites first.

In v.16 he states the bad news that not all of the Jewish
people obeyed the good news, that is, believed. The quotation from Isaiah (54:1) is a rhetorical question implying a
negative response. If Paul was aware when he quoted this
that it was from one of the poems concerning the "suffering
servant of Yahweh," then he would have seen it as especially
appropriate for the good news of the crucified and risen
Christ. Paul makes explicit the Christian application of the
quotation by a rather awkward reference to "the preaching
of Christ" (v.17). The Greek word for "preaching" can also
be translated "word" or "message." One of those would seem
to be more appropriate since the context is dealing with the
apostolic preaching, not Christ's.

The objection cannot be made that the Jewish people have
not heard the gospel. The best argument against that would
really be the historical experience. Jesus' mission was almost
exclusively to his own people, and the Christian missionaries in Paul's time always preached in the synagogues
first. But Paul probably just takes that experience for
granted and indulges his rabbinic penchant for quoting a
text from Scripture as the best argument (v.18). He quotes
Ps 19:4 which, for the psalmist, refers to creation's voice
praising God throughout the world. Paul uses it as a reference to the historical experience mentioned above. If even
Rome, the center of the civilized world, heard the message,
then surely Israel did, too.

The objection that they heard but did not understand is
refuted by another Scripture quote, this one from Dt 32:21,
which is a bit more appropriate (v.19). There, Moses was
saying that Israel would be made jealous by a pagan nation.
Paul, of course, means that if the Gentiles understood and
believed, there is all the more reason why Israel should have.
The same point is made by the prophet (Is 65:1) in a slightly
different form (v.20). The Gentiles, who weren't even looking for the message, found and accepted it. Then, in one
final reference to the Scriptures (Is 62:2, the same passage as

in the preceding verse), the apostle cites the reason for Israel's stumbling as forcefully as possible (v.21). Preachers were sent, they preached the message, Israel heard the message, she must have understood it, but being "disobedient and contrary," she did not accept it.

THE MYSTERY RESOLVED.
11:1-36.

The closing verse of chapter 10 would seem to have resolved the mystery of Judaism: disobedience has brought final rejection. But that is far from Paul's way of thinking, as he has already intimated (3:1-4). He says that much more forthrightly in this chapter. First of all, not all of the people have been rejected (vv.1-10). Secondly, the conversion of the Gentiles can be seen as a preparation for that of all Israel (vv.11-24). Thirdly, the resolution of the mystery is seen in God's mercy being extended to all (vv.25-36).

> **11** I ask, then, has God rejected his people? By no means! I myself am an Israelite, a descendant of Abraham, a member of the tribe of Benjamin. ²God has not rejected his people whom he foreknew. Do you not know what the scripture says of Elijah, how he pleads with God against Israel? ³"Lord, they have killed thy prophets, they have demolished thy altars, and I alone am left, and they seek my life." ⁴But what is God's reply to him? "I have kept for myself seven thousand men who have not bowed the knee to Baal." ⁵So too at the present time there is a remnant, chosen by grace. ⁶But if it is by grace, it is no longer on the basis of works; otherwise grace would no longer be grace.
>
> ⁷What then? Israel failed to obtain what it sought. The elect obtained it, but the rest were hardened, ⁸as it is written, "God gave them a spirit of stupor, eyes that should not see and ears that should not hear, down to this very day." ⁹And David says, "Let their table become a snare and a trap, a pitfall and a retribution for them, ¹⁰let their eyes be darkened so that they cannot see, and bend their backs for ever."

Paul begins this first section by asking the question that would naturally be asked after the preceding verse (10:21): have God's own people been rejected? His explosive "no" is immediately followed by his first, and very personal, argument. He himself is a Jew, from the loins of Abraham, and a member of the prestigious tribe of Benjamin that fathered Israel's first king, Saul, Paul's namesake. While it can be argued, on the basis of Paul's own line of argument throughout the letter, that he, Paul, was not elected because he was a Jew (that would suggest a human motivation for the divine choice, a form of works righteousness), still the fact that a Jew was chosen, and to be an apostle, even if the least of all (1 Cor 15:8-9), is incontrovertible evidence that God has not rejected all of Israel. V.2a, which mirrors Ps 94:14 and recalls what he himself said in 8:29, doesn't seem to be just a repetition of his contention in v. 1, but, by reason of the addition of "whom he foreknew," another argument. God's foreknowledge includes predestination to be conformed to the Son's image (8:29). (We must keep in mind that, as generally in statements of this nature, Paul is thinking of the people, the collective, rather than of individuals.).

Still another argument against total rejection is the case of Elijah (vv.2-4). This prophet of the northern kingdom is thought by some scholars to have been the major reason for the preservation of Israelite religion in the north. Yet so intense was the royal persecution against him that he thought that he alone remained as a true worshiper, and his life was sought (1 Kg 19:10). But God assured him that there were seven thousand Israelites who had not worshipped the Canaanite pagan god, Baal. The point Paul is making here is one familiar to the people from the Old Testament, especially Isaiah (10:20-22; 11:11, 16), namely, that a mere remnant can be the source for the ultimate fulfillment of God's original intention. The remnant, too, of course, exists by grace, not by reason of any "works" or merits of its own. But this only enhances the hope of ultimate salvation for all, since the hope rests in God, not in Israel (vv.5-6).

In vv.7 to 10 Paul goes back to a consideration of the
"non-elect," the "non-remnant," those who "were hardened." The passages quoted in vv.8-10, from Is 29:10 and Ps
69:22-23, are still more examples of the biblical manner of
expressing divine sovereignty and of its failure to distinguish
between God's absolute and permissive will (cf. comments
on 9:17-18). More importantly, Paul brings up this dreary
subject again to prepare for his major stroke in the following section. Things do not look good for Israel: will they
really be slaves ("bend their backs") for ever?

> [11]So I ask, have they stumbled so as to fall? By no
> means! But through their trespass, salvation has come to
> the Gentiles, so as to make Israel jealous. [12]Now if their
> trespass means riches for the world, and if their failure
> means riches for the Gentiles, how much more will their
> full inclusion mean!

> [13]Now I am speaking to you Gentiles. Inasmuch then
> as I am an apostle to the Gentiles, I magnify my ministry
> [14]in order to make my fellow Jews jealous, and thus save
> some of them. [15]For if their rejection means the reconcilia-
> tion of the world, what will their acceptance mean but life
> from the dead? [16]If the dough offered as first fruits is holy,
> so is the whole lump; and if the root is holy, so are the
> branches.

> [17]But if some of the branches were broken off, and you,
> a wild olive shoot, were grafted in their place to share
> the richness of the olive tree, [18]do not boast over the
> branches. If you do boast, remember it is not you that
> support the root, but the root that supports you. [19]You
> will say, "Branches were broken off so that I might be
> grafted in." [20]That is true. They were broken off because
> of their unbelief, but you stand fast only through faith.
> So do not become proud, but stand in awe. [21]For if God
> did not spare the natural branches, neither will he spare

you. ²²Note then the kindness and the severity of God: severity toward those who have fallen, but God's kindness to you, provided you continue in his kindness; otherwise you too will be cut off. ²³And even the others, if they do not persist in their unbelief, will be grafted in, for God has the power to graft them in again. ²⁴For if you have been cut from what is by nature a wild olive tree, and grafted, contrary to nature, into a cultivated olive tree, how much more will these natural branches be grafted back into their own olive tree.

So, Paul has argued that the salvation of a remnant proves that all Israel has not been rejected. But what of those, clearly the majority, who have "stumbled" by not accepting Christ? Have they fallen (presumably forever)? Again we have the same explosive "no" as in v.1. In v.11b we have a compact summary of his argument in this section: Israel's trespass led to the Gentiles' salvation which in turn will move Israel to faith (that is the implication of her "jealousy"). If her "trespass" or "failure" brings riches to others, how much more will the reverse bring (v.12)! The reverse, of course, is their "inclusion" in God's saving plan which will attain its full complement of those saved.

The reference to Gentiles in v.13 suggests for many scholars that the majority of the Roman Christians were converts from paganism. Paul has elsewhere (v.g. 1:13) emphasized his ministry to the Gentiles. He repeats it here and even boasts of it (v.13b). But then he adds a strange note. He has exercised this ministry for the real purpose of bringing at least some of the Jews to conversion through their jealousy of the Gentiles' faith (v.14). This must not be understood, however, as meaning that "he has, ultimately and at bottom, only Israel's rescue in mind" (Schelkle). The Roman Christians would hardly accept that with equanimity. Rather, it is a typical Pauline exaggeration to emphasize that, despite his special apostolate to the Gentiles, he is also concerned about his own people. At bottom he is concerned about the salvation of all (v.32).

In v. 15 he returns to the thought of v. 12 and repeats it in a more striking way. If the Jewish rejection of Christ means (and this should be interpreted as "has occasioned") the reconciliation of the world (perhaps a reference to the future conversion of all Gentiles), then the future acceptance of Christ by the Jews will mean the ultimate good, "life from the dead." If Paul is thinking here of the end-time, then "life from the dead" could well mean the general resurrection of the dead that will then take place. Thus, the order in Paul's mind would be: rejection of Christ by the Jews, acceptance by the Gentiles, acceptance by the Jews, the general resurrection. And he does like to think in an ordered sequence such as this (cf. 1 Cor 15:20-28 for a strong illustration). This thinking in sequence encourages him to introduce the note of causality in the events (one event happens *in order that* the next event might take place), where we would rather speak of one event as the occasion for another, or where we would simply say that one follows the other without suggesting a relationship. But for Paul, with his strong belief in divine providence, nothing happens by chance; there is always a God-willed relation between events. Many would hold that "life from the dead" simply means that Israel, once dead in disbelief, has now come to the life of faith. The other explanation, however, seems more in keeping with the parallel "reconciliation of the world."

In v. 16 Paul seems to be striking a new note. He is not speaking here of the future condition of Israel but of her present condition, and his general principle, in the two figures, is that a holy part sanctifies the remainder. In the first figure of the first fruits, he is alluding to Num 15:18-21 where the part of the grain is offered to God as a symbol of the offering of all of it to him. But of whom is Paul writing here? Some think these "first fruits" are the patriarchs to whom the promises were originally made and for the sake of whom all Israel was loved by God (cf. Dt 7:7-8). Others argue that Paul is thinking here of the "remnant," the Jews already converted who are the first of all to be made holy. The second figure of the root and branches can also be understood in both ways. In the light of what follows (cf. v.18) it seems best to understand the root here to refer to Israel of old, especially the patriarchs. The branches then would represent all their physical descendants. In any case the meaning is that there is holiness in Israel and it will lead to more holiness.

The second figure is now developed by Paul (vv.17-24). The disbelieving Jews are the branches broken off, and the Gentiles are the "wild olive shoot" grafted on to the (obviously still living) trunk (v.17). This leads Paul to what must have been an unexpected conclusion, at least for the Romans if not for most Christians today. Gentile Christians do not support Israel; Israel supports the Gentile Christians (v.18). The apostle makes this profound observation in the context of a reminder to the Romans that they should not boast of their situation, which suggests that there may have been some anti-Semitism among them. If there was, v.18 is a healthy corrective to them as to all Christians.

The objection voiced in v.19 suggests, again, a causality between broken branches and engrafted branches: Israel is broken off in order that Gentiles might be grafted in. And Paul seems to agree with this in v.20a. But in the rest of that verse he says something else. Her disbelief caused her to be broken off, and the Gentiles' faith caused them to replace them. So the note of causality in v.19 is not to be taken literally. And what is more to the point is that if the Romans are grafted in by reason of the gift of faith, that must preclude any boasting. Faith and boasting are mutually exclusive. They can stand in wonder at the mysteriousness of God's providence, but they cannot take any credit for it.

Another note is struck. Not only should the Romans not boast, they should beware of sharing the natural branches' fate (v.21). God's kindness, manifested in the Romans' faith, demands a response of perseverance or it can be experienced as his severity (v.22). In the same way, God's severity, now experienced by the disbelievers, will be turned to kindness if they believe (v.23). Thus, the wild branches, grafted in, can be broken off, and the natural branches, broken off, can be grafted in again. In fact, Paul concludes, it is all the easier for the natural branches to be restored, since it was "contrary to nature" that the wild branches were grafted into the cultivated tree (v.24). He ends this section, then, by painting a very optimistic picture of Israel's situation in the future.

> ²⁵Lest you be wise in your own conceits, I want you to understand this mystery, brethren: a hardening has come upon part of Israel, until the full number of the Gentiles come in, ²⁶and so all Israel will be saved; as it is written,
> "The Deliverer will come from Zion,
>   he will banish ungodliness from Jacob";
> ²⁷"and this will be my covenant with them
>   when I take away their sins."
> ²⁸As regards the gospel they are enemies of God, for your sake; but as regards election they are beloved for the sake of their forefathers. ²⁹For the gifts and the call of God are irrevocable. ³⁰Just as you were once disobedient to God but now have received mercy because of their disobedience, ³¹so they have now been disobedient in order that by the mercy shown to you they also may receive mercy. ³²For God has consigned all men to disobedience, that he may have mercy upon all.
> ³³O the depth of the riches and wisdom and knowledge of God! How unsearchable are his judgments and how inscrutable his ways!
> ³⁴"For who has known the mind of the Lord,
>   or who has been his counselor?"
> ³⁵"Or who has given a gift to him
>   that he might be repaid?"
> ³⁶For from him and through him and to him are all things. To him be glory for ever. Amen.

In this final passage Paul becomes even more optimistic in his evaluation of Israel's status in God's sight. One can almost see him struggling and praying as he writes. He now uses the highly charged theological word "mystery" to describe the problem of Israel's situation. For Paul "mystery" refers to the core of God's salvific plan (cf. 1 Cor 2:7; 4:1) which has been revealed only in the Christian era and to a chosen few that they might bring it to the world. The mystery is that Israel's "hardening" is only temporary; it will come to an end when all those Gentiles who will be converted are converted (this is probably the only way to interpret the "full number") (v.25). Their conversion is the religious condition, not just a chronological signpost (Paul says "and so," not "and then"), for Israel's conversion, a point he had spelled out previously (cf. vv.11, 19-20). Citing a mixture of Is 59:20-21 and 27:9, he finds a basis for this conversion in the Old Testament (vv.26-27).

The Jews, as a whole, have rejected the good news of Jesus Christ, only recently manifested, and, in this respect, they have to be said to be enemies of God, a condition redounding to the Gentiles' benefit (v.28a). But their earlier election as God's people in fulfillment of the promises to the patriarchs still constitutes them as "beloved" in God's sight (v.28b). God doesn't give and then take back (v.29). This puts Israel in the very ambiguous situation of election-rejection, both of which are maintained. That is why Paul must conclude that the present rejection has to be terminated. And he does this, again, by linking the (temporary) disobedience of Israel with the conversion of the Gentiles (v.30). Once God's mercy has been demonstrated in the latter event, it will be demonstrated in Israel's ultimate conversion, (v.31). And he sums it all up by saying that human disobedience is only a temporary factor in God's plan to manifest his universal will for salvation (v.32).

In 1 Cor 3:21-23 Paul had concluded his remarks on factions in the Church with a beautiful statement on the meaning of all things for the Christians in the larger, all-enveloping context of Christ and God. In our letter, in 8:38-39, he bursts forth with a concluding and universal statement on the power of the bond of love between God and the

Christian. In much the same way he now sums up his praying and struggling over the question of Judaism with a hymn to God's unsearchable wisdom and ways (vv.33-36). While he surely must hope that he has given some insights into a terribly complex problem, he knows that there are no final human answers. Put as simply as possible, that is so because God is God. The prophets of old had already expressed the impossibility of fathoming the Lord's mind (Is 40:13), and the wise man had declared the divine refusal to barter away his plans (cf. Job 35:7; 41:11). If we believe that this God is a God of love, then the conviction that absolutely everything comes from him, has its meaning in him, and is destined for him can only be a supreme consolation in the face of all mystery (v.36a). In that light one can only give him glory and profess one's faith with a resounding "Amen" (v.36b).

THE CHRISTIAN WAY TO LIVE.
12:1 - 15:13

Having concluded his side excursion on the question of Judaism, Paul now takes up where he had left off at the conclusion of c.8. There he had spoken of the new life Christians enjoy in Christ and in the Spirit. That had been made possible through the gift of faith. Now he wants to indicate the consequences of that new life, the human response to the divine gift. The close association of these two, gift and response, should be kept in mind because Christian morality cannot be reduced to a philosophical system. Rather, it flows from the power and the wonder of what God has done in us. That is why it will never be as predictable as a philosophical conclusion. In this follow-up, then, to what he had said previously, Paul writes of the Christian way to life in response to God's saving action.

UNION AND LOVE.
12:1-21

After an initial general statement on the Christian's relationship to God and the world (vv.1-2), he describes the union of Christian with Christian in the Body of Christ and their interdependence by reason of the diversity of their gifts (vv.3-8). He then shows the myriad ways in which we can show our love for one another (vv.9-21).

> **12** I appeal to you therefore, brethren, by the mercies of God, to present your bodies as a living sacrifice, holy and

> acceptable to God, which is your spiritual worship. ²Do
> not be conformed to this world but be transformed by the
> renewal of your mind, that you may prove what is the will
> of God, what is good and acceptable and perfect.

Paul begins with an appeal to the Romans that finds its motivation in God's "mercies." While he must be referring in part to the "mercy" (a different word in Greek) mentioned in 11:30 to 32, he doubtless had in mind all that God had done and which the apostle had described in the preceding chapters. They are asked to make their "bodies," that is, their very selves as human beings, completely available to God (v. 1). Paul extols such an action in many ways. A "sacrifice" basically suggests a complete offering, a consecration that removes the object sacrificed from the possession of the offerer. It is a "living" sacrifice because the Christian retains life; the sacrifice is not effected, as it usually is, through the death of the victim. Such an offering becomes, for Christians, their "spiritual worship." The Greek word translated "spiritual" is *logikos*, which is literally "logical" or "what might be reasonably expected." But Paul is speaking here of a divine "logic" that probes more deeply than human reason. So he is not speaking of a worship whose central act is a material sacrifice, but one, as we have seen, which is characterized by human consecration. Therefore the "logic" of this worship is of the spirit, or "spiritual."

Continuing with his general observations, he writes of the kind of conformity that should mark the Christian (v.2). It is not to the "world," that is, the old age dominated by sin which is still very alive and active. But the Christian must be conformed to the new age which has already been inaugurated through Christ. The two ages, or "worlds," therefore, co-exist, but "the end of the ages" has come upon Christians (1 Cor 10:11). This can also be expressed, as here, by a transformation marked by a newness of the inner self. In all this Paul seems to be speaking primarily of the action of God in the human person who through faith has opened the inner self to his action. When this opening takes place, through the sacrificial offering of our bodies, through conformity to the new age, through the newness of one's being, then the Christians can determine God's will, namely, what is the best thing to do in all ways, because, in a sense, it is God who is making the determination in them.

> ³For by the grace given to me I bid every one among you not to think of himself more highly than he ought to think, but to think with sober judgment, each according to the measure of faith which God has assigned him. ⁴For as in one body we have many members, and all the members do not have the same function, ⁵so we, though many, are one body in Christ, and individually members of one another. ⁶Having gifts that differ according to the grace given to us, let us use them: if prophecy, in proportion to our faith; ⁷if service, in our serving; he who teaches, in his teaching; ⁸he who exhorts, in his exhortation; he who contributes, in liberality; he who gives aid, with zeal; he who does acts of mercy, with cheerfulness.

Since ethical conduct is expected of the Christian as a necessary consequence of the openness to God's saving work, some principles for that conduct must be laid down. The first one has to do with the proper use of one's own talents and abilities, really, one's "gifts," as Paul calls them, because they are, ultimately, from God. But Paul sees these natural talents and abilities as having a new dimension by reason of the Christian faith, and so they are "gifts" in a new way also. The first thing that must be said about these gifts is that they be accepted and exercised in the proper perspective. The early Christian communities, like ours today, were plagued with individualism, according to which individual Christians tended to seek their own personal fulfillment without a proper concern for the community as a whole. At least that was a problem in the Corinthian community (cf. 1 Cor 12-14) and it could possibly surface in the Roman community. It is why the apostle has to insist that individuals not think too highly of themselves and that they judge their gifts "according to the measure of faith" assigned them by God (v.3). "Faith" here is clearly not the justifying faith of the earlier chapters. Rather, it refers to what they believe, the doctrinal emergent of their act of surrender to God. If they judge in accord with that faith, it should be a sound and balanced judgment. Thus, Paul's "grace," as an apostle, is to remind others of their obligations in this regard (v.3a).

He uses as an analogy for an interdependence of these gifts the human body, which he had already used in his Corinthian correspondence for the same purpose (1 Cor 12:12-30). Each member of the body has its own proper function (v.4) and each has to work in harmony with the others. Christians similarly form one body in Christ. This Christ dimension not only encourages but even demands unity and cooperation among the members (v.5).

Paul then mentions some of the gifts. It is doubtful that the order of their appearance has significance. More important is that their diversity shows that he is thinking here of Christians *as* Christians, and not as necessarily exercising any hierarchial role. The first mentioned is prophecy (v.6), which is "inspired utterance" (NEB) or the forceful proclamation of the word. It can include prediction at times (cf. Acts 21:10-11). "Our faith" here is the common belief of Christians. The second gift is "service" (*diakonia*), possibly the more menial tasks (v.7). The third, teaching, is the more formal Christian instruction. The fourth, exhortation, means encouragement and consolation. Then follows the giving of alms which should be done for no selfish purpose. The sixth gift, according to RSV, is the "giving of aid;" the Greek can also mean "presiding" as an official in the community. This seems preferable. The "zeal" of the official is also said to characterize Titus (2 Cor 8:16), (translated "earnest care" in RSV). The final gift, doing "acts of mercy," is to be exercised with a cheerful forgetfulness of self (v.8).

⁹Let love be genuine; hate what is evil, hold fast to what is good; ¹⁰love one another with brotherly affection; outdo one another in showing honor. ¹¹Never flag in zeal, be aglow with the Spirit, serve the Lord. ¹²Rejoice in your hope, be patient in tribulation, be constant in prayer. ¹³Contribute to the needs of the saints, practice hospitality.

¹⁴Bless those who persecute you; bless and do not curse them. ¹⁵Rejoice with those who rejoice, weep with those who weep. ¹⁶Live in harmony with one another; do not be haughty, but associate with the lowly; never be conceited. ¹⁷Repay no one evil for evil, but take thought for what is noble in the sight of all. ¹⁸If possible, so far as it depends upon you. live peaceably with all. ¹⁹Beloved, never avenge yourselves, but leave it to the wrath of God; for it is written, "Vengeance is mine, I will repay, says the Lord." ²⁰No, "if your enemy is hungry, feed him; if he is thirsty, give him a drink; for by so doing you will heap burning coals upon his head." ²¹Do not be overcome by evil, but overcome evil with good.

With v.9 Paul begins a series of terse sayings which embody basic truths about Christian attitudes. Each one could stand on its own, somewhat like the individual proverbs of OT, several of which he refers to here. Two general observations can be made about this series. First of all, the apostle is very much aware of the presence of evil in the world and of the need for the Christians to overcome it. This is why he begins the series with love, which for him is not only the greatest of the gifts (cf. 1 Cor 12:31-13:13) but the key to all Christian ethics (Rom 13:8-10). Secondly, his principles treat of Christians' attitudes to other Christians (vv.9-13, 15-16) and to non-Christians, especially to enemies (vv.14, 17-21). Other than that there is no intrinsic unity to the series, although it can be seen how one saying may have occasioned another. We need not think that Paul created all of these sayings, but the fact that he brought together in one place so many radical principles is creative in itself.

As noted, he begins with love (v.9). To say that it must be "genuine" (literally "unhypocritical") is really repetitious, as true love (*agapē*) is such by nature. But Paul is aware that we often claim as an act of love something that is ultimately self-serving; that is not genuine and it is not love. Genuine love, then, means repudiating or abhorring what is evil and remaining fastened to what is good. While Christianity demands love of everyone, even enemies, it is understandable that there should be a special affection for other Christians (*philadelphia*, "brotherly love"). With respect to these there will be a special effort made to show them honor (v.10). "Zeal" (v.11) involves an eagerness or sense of urgency, which suggests the principle behind this, namely, the Holy Spirit who sets us aglow. "Serve the Lord" is much too prosaic an injunction in this context. Why would Paul add such an obvious command in this highly charged passage? Some good manuscripts have an alternative reading, which is very close in the Greek (*kairō* for *kyriō*), and which means that they are to recognize "the opportune time" in which they live and act accordingly. In other words, he is saying here in a brief phrase what he will spell out more clearly in 13:11-13. V.12 contains familiar Pauline themes; they can all be understood more readily in a context of adversity, even persecution, though that is not a supposed background of the letter. In a more pragmatic vein he encourages a renewed sense of meeting other Christians' needs and especially of welcoming them, even though unknown (*philoxenia*; cf. *philadelphia* in v.10), into their homes (v.13).

With v.14 we have the first of his injunctions on relating to enemies, and it is a strong one. Christians must "bless" them. This is not just a weak "fare-thee-well," but implies an actual prayer to God for their welfare. In the Semitic mind a word of blessing, if genuine, goes forth from the speaker into the person blessed and already has some effect. Paul repeats the charge. This is no less than what Jesus expects of his followers in the Mount Sermon (Mt 5:44). Reverting to less specific objects of concern in v.15, he asks that they be sympathetic to others, whether in joy or sorrow (cf. Sir 7:34).

This is one more indication that Christianity, far from being a denial of humanism, is really its most radical champion. In v. 16 the four injunctions are intimately related. The first states the general, positive principle of equal regard for all. The second guards against an undue regard for "higher things," while the third urges special concern for the lowly (whether prsons or things is uncertain). The fourth sums it up in a negative way by cautioning against an inflated notion of one's self. The point is that, if we have an honest picture of ourselves before God, we should have no difficulty in relating to others.

The final verses (17-21) deal, again, with the Christian attitude to evil-doers. And the first principle enunciated here is a basic one, repeated in a positive form in v. 21, but a principle that is one of the most difficult for human beings to live by. Jesus had urged it in the Sermon (Mt 5:38-41). Retaliation is not a Christian approach to evil (v. 17a). The injunction is somewhat weakened by the following one placed in such close proximity. But it is related: we must let others, even enemies, see the "noble," or the ethical good, in us. In v. 18 Paul becomes almost apologetic about the injunction's positive implications, saying equivalently that we must do our best to live in peace with all. This is an understandable reservation because true peace presupposes a positive attitude on the part of both parties. Christians can be responsible only for their own attitude.

In accord with the principle of v. 17a, vengeance, too, is necessarily excluded (v. 19). That vengeance is the Lord's is an Old Testament principle (Dt 32:35), although Christians would understand it in a slightly different way. God has so ordered the world that evil finds its own punishment (cf. comments on 1:18). We are not capable of addressing, much less satisfying for, evil. "We are neither wise enough nor good enough to punish our enemies justly" (note in *The New Oxford Annotated Bible*). The recommendation in v. 20 is a classical *crux interpretum* ("interpreters' cross"); it has yet to yield a completely satisfactory interpretation. Based on

Proverbs 25:21-22, it urges charity, in a pragmatic way, toward one's enemies, a perfectly intelligible action in view of Jesus' love command (Mt 5:43-48). The best that can be said about the "burning coals" is that they may suggest the shame experienced by those who are the objects of such charitable deeds.

The final injunction (v.21) is a powerful and radical insight into the problem of evil. It is so radical that relatively few have been able to understand, much less abide by it. The normal human reaction is to confront evil with evil in order to avoid being overcome by it. Violence must be met with violence. The killer must be killed. The hater must be hated. In the face of this common attitude Paul breaks through with the paradoxical command that we be victorious over evil by doing good.

THE CHRISTIAN IN THE "NOW" WORLD. 13:1-14.

Having proposed a series of principles indicating basic attitudes that Christians should have, Paul gives some specific instructions on how to conduct oneself in the "now" world, that is, a world that goes about its daily routine with the usual structures, but a world that, for the Christian, has also been transformed by the Christ event. With respect, then, to the "now" world, Christians must know how to respond to civil authority (vv. 1-7), how love can provide a key to one's relation to the neighbor (vv.8-10), and what to do in the light of the "end of the ages" (1 Cor 10:11) that has come upon us (vv.11-14).

> **13** Let every person be subject to the governing authorities. For there is no authority except from God, and those that exist have been instituted by God. [2]Therefore he who resists the authorities resists what God has appointed, and those who resist will incur judgment. [3]For rulers are not a terror to good conduct, but to bad. Would you have

no fear of him who is in authority? Then do what is good, and you will receive his approval, ⁴for he is God's servant for your good. But if you do wrong, be afraid, for he does not bear the sword in vain; he is the servant of God to execute his wrath on the wrongdoer. ⁵Therefore one must be subject, not only to avoid God's wrath but also for the sake of conscience. ⁶For the same reason you also pay taxes, for the authorities are ministers of God, attending to this very thing. ⁷Pay all of them their dues, taxes to whom taxes are due, revenue to whom revenue is due, respect to whom respect is due, honor to whom honor is due.

In one sense Paul's remarks on civil obedience are startling. Elsewhere he had remarked that "our commonwealth is in heaven" (Phil 3:20), which might suggest at best a neutral attitude toward secular government. Also, Paul himself had suffered at the hands of these authorities, though not yet at Rome (2 Cor 11:23-27). The Acts of the Apostles record some of the violence visited by them on him (cf. 16:19-24). He would have known the responsibility of the Roman authorities for the death of Jesus. And he testifies himself to the incongruity of a Christian taking another Christian to the secular court of law (1 Cor 6:1-6). Yet, in this section he reveals a very positive attitude to secular government, allowing that it is of divine institution and so having divine sanction.

There are several factors, however, that help to explain the apostle's instructions here. The Jews in their own long history had seen God as acknowledging, even choosing the king who would rule over his people (1 Sam 10:1, 16:1-13). Moreover, a prophet of the exile could envision a pagan ruler being anointed by God to lead his people to freedom (Is 45:1-3). At a later date, the author of Daniel has the prophet announce that it is God who gave the kingdom and the power to rule to Nebuchadnezzar (2:37-38). Still later, shortly before the time of Jesus, the Jewish author of Wisdom warns all the kings and judges "of the ends of the earth" that it is God who has given them dominion and to him they are accountable (6:1-11).

It is not likely that Paul was unaware of this rich tradition. It would have been theologically normal for him to have accepted the divine hand behind the legitimate authorities. If he includes no warning against the abuse of power, it must be because he was not aware of any in Rome. It has been pointed out that from 54 to 62 the administration of the Empire was pretty much under the control of Seneca, the court philosopher, and the later tyranny of Nero had not yet manifested itself. And Paul himself apparently was confident enough to have made, at a later date, the appeal of a Roman citizen to Caesar for an adjudication of his case (Acts 25:11-12). What Paul has to say here, then, should not be all that surprising. It simply should not be seen as an absolute statement binding in all details for all times without exception. He himself would certainly say what Peter is recorded as having said, "We must obey God rather than men" (Acts 5:29). In fact, as we shall see, he does leave the door open for that kind of evaluation of secular power.

The general principle is enunciated in v.1. Authority is from God and so demands respect and, indeed, submission to it. The plural, "authorities," refers to those who actually exercise the power. The word "governing" could also be translated "supreme;" it simply designates those who are in a higher position than others. An obvious presupposition of this principle is that the authority is legitimate. But this is not stated because there was no need to question, on Paul's part, the legitimacy of Rome's authority. It is legitimate (supposed); therefore it is from God. The first part of v.2 flows naturally from the principle. The only question about the second part is whether the judgment incurred is from God or from the authorities. In the context of this verse alone it could be both, and in a sense it is. But in the larger context it is clear that Paul has the human authorities primarily in mind.

Granted, again, the legitimacy of the rulers, they are an occasion of fear only in the situation of bad conduct which disrupts the order of society. So, if anyone wishes to avoid such fear, it is only necessary to act in accord with the rules of society which are ordered to the common good. Not only is there the satisfaction of doing good, but there will also be praise from the authority. This latter should not be seen as the principal motivating force envisioned by Paul, but simply as an expected recognition, in the name of the whole society, of some special good done (v.3). In the following verse the sanction of punishment, even the death sentence, is clearly set forth. While it is interesting to speculate on how Paul would argue in today's context of the capital punishment debate, he could not have seen it in his day any differently than he did the institution of slavery. It was part of the fixed order of things to which the Christ event could make occasional exception (cf. Philem). In rewarding the good or in punishing the evil, the authority is God's servant.

Almost all commentators see v.5 as introducing a new and significant element into the presentation, namely, the matter of conscience. Once one admits that the individual conscience has a say in the matter, then the opening is there for a conscientious disobedience of civil authority. Paul clearly does not envision it here. In fact, he sees conscience here as confirming the actions of the authorities. But once the moral judgment of the individual is made a criterion of action, then the penal law is no longer the sole criterion and pure legalism is excluded.

The "same reason" of v.6 is probably both the fear of God's wrath and conscience's sake. Both justify the payment of taxes. Paul was quite likely aware of Jesus' statement on this same subject (Mk 12:17). Despite the resistance of the Jewish Zealots and some of the Pharisees to this practice, it would seem, from the way Paul writes, that the Roman Christians were paying whatever taxes were required of them. It is not certain whether Paul was aware of the precise distinction between the two kinds of taxes he mentions (v.7).

(The translations vary: "taxes" and "revenue" in RSV; "direct tax" and "indirect" in JB; "taxes" and "toll" in NAB and NEB; "personal and property taxes" in TEV.) Respect the established order is the sum of it.

> [8]Owe no one anything, except to love one another; for he who loves his neighbor has fulfilled the law. [9]The commandments, "You shall not commit adultery, You shall not kill, You shall not steal, You shall not covet," and any other commandment, are summed up in this sentence, "You shall love your neighbor as yourself." [10]Love does no wrong to a neighbor; therefore love is the fulfilling of the law.

This passage is not totally independent of the preceding. The "dues" of v.7 and the "owe" of v.8 are from the same Greek root. It is typical of biblical literature to use such "catch words" to indicate a continuity of theme. In other words, what is "owed" to the government reminds Paul of something far more important that all Christians "owe" to others, that is, love. His basic thesis is that if we pay the debt of love, we will by necesisty do all else that must be done for others. Thus love "fulfills the law" in the sense that every commandment that can be conceived will be obeyed if we love others. To put it in other terms, if we love others, we will do nothing to hurt them. And hurting them is precisely what the commandments forbid. Paul cites some of the major commandments to make his point, cited in an order found in some ancient manuscripts.

Today there are some who would say that the Ten Commandments are no longer valid; they have been set aside by the commandment of love. But from what has just been said it is clear that the commandment of love is another and more positive way of expressing the Ten Commandments. The latter have not been set aside by that of love; they have been fulfilled by it.

Jesus, of course, had already summed up the whole law in the two-fold commandment to love God and neighbor (Mk 12:28-31). It is most important to note that this command to love is given by God himself, and he alone is capable of giving such a command because he alone can empower a person to love. The significance of this is realized when we imagine one human person commanding another to love. A human person can command another not to kill or steal or commit adultery and enforce the commandment. But the interior act of love, which then conditions all external actions, can only be commanded by God who makes is possible.

> [11]Besides this you know what hour it is, how it is full time now for you to wake from sleep. For salvation is nearer to us now than when we first believed; [12]the night is far gone, the day is at hand. Let us then cast off the works of darkness and put on the armor of light; [13]let us conduct ourselves becomingly as in the day, not in reveling and drunkenness, not in debauchery and licentiousness, not in quarreling and jealousy. [14]But put on the Lord Jesus Christ, and make no provision for the flesh, to gratify its desires.

From the requirements of the civil law (vv.1-7) Paul had passed to the much more profound requirements of love (vv.8-10). Now he treats of the requirements that are evoked by the end-time, the new age which has been inaugurated by the Christ event and which is pointing ineluctably to consummation, to the fullness of God's kingdom. A number of words in this passage, besides the general tenor, betray this sense of eschatological urgency: "hour," "time," "now," "the day," "light" are all terms used by Paul and others when speaking of the end-time, and they have a special, charged meaning when so used. Behind all of this and explaining it is the conviction that the Lord Jesus Christ is coming in his second and glorious coming to usher in God's kingdom in its fullness. In his earlier writings Paul thought that this would take place in his own lifetime (cf. 1 Thess 4:15-17). Later he writes in a spirit that shows he could envision his own death before this event (Phil 1:21-23). But he never lost a sense of the imminence of the Lord's coming (cf. 1 Cor 7:26, 29-31). This is evident in our present passage also.

"Waking from sleep" (v.11) is a natural enough symbol for becoming aware of what is transpiring. And ordinarily this is done when day approaches, which for Paul means the day of the Lord's coming. "Salvation" here is taken in the fullest sense of complete possession of the kingdom. Thus, while Paul could and did occasionally speak of salvation in the present (Rom 8:24; 1 Cor 1:18), this was only an incipient salvation that awaited consummation in the Lord's coming. And he is convinced that this fulness of salvation is "nearer" than when they first believed. This is not easy to understand. He surely does not mean that each morning, when they awake, they are twenty-four hours closer to the *parousia.* He is not reckoning time in that way. It can only mean that, as we grow in our faith, the certainty of our hope in the *parousia* grows stronger and impresses itself upon us more and more as an imminent event. We must speak, then, of a theological or religious imminence rather than of a chronological one. And in this sense Paul's words have as much meaning for us today as they did for the Romans. Night is the time for the "works of darkness" in a moral sense (v.12). The Roman Christians have, supposedly, already renounced these, but there is always the need to renew our resolutions to "put on the armor of light." The imagery of "putting on" something to indicate a new personality or a new characteristic is frequent in the Scriptures (Is 11:5; Ps 132:9) and especially in Paul's letters (v.g. 1 Cor 15:53, 54, 2 Cor 5:3). Here "the armor of light" symbolizes the virtues that can protect us from the assault of evil. This is spelled out in a negative way in v.13 by the mentioning of the vices to be avoided. The majority of the vices are exactly those which are wont to be practiced at night time. He concludes with a strong statement about putting on "the Lord Jesus Christ." This shows the different ways in which Paul can look on the Christian movement. In Gal 3:27 he reminds his readers that they *have* put on Christ in baptism. There is a sense in which salvation has been realized. Here, in telling Roman Christians to put on Christ, he indicates there is a sense in which salvation is yet to be realized.

LIVING DIFFERENTLY IN HARMONY. 14:1-12.

In the entire passage, from 14:1 to 15:13, Paul is talking about harmonious relations among the Christians of Rome. There were differences in the practices of eating certain foods and observing certain days. A similar problem had arisen in the church at Corinth (cf. 1 Cor 8-10), where the letter to Rome was being written. Perhaps he is basing his discussion on that experience. In any case, his main concern here is that everyone respect the consciences of the others in these matters. It should be added here that some recent commentators hold that Rom 14:1-15:13 is not directed to a specific situation in Rome but simply reflects Paul's moral theology as developed also in 1 Cor 8-10.

> **14** As for the man who is weak in faith, welcome him, but not for disputes over opinions. ²One believes he may eat anything, while the weak man eats only vegetables. ³Let not him who eats despise him who abstains, and let not him who abstains pass judgment on him who eats; for God has welcomed him. ⁴Who are you to pass judgment on the servant of another? It is before his own master that he stands or falls. And he will be upheld, for the Master is able to make him stand.
>
> ⁵One man esteems one day as better than another, while another man esteems all days alike. Let every one be fully convinced in his own mind. ⁶He who observes the day, observes it in honor of the Lord. He also who eats, eats in honor of the Lord, since he gives thanks to God; while he

who abstains, abstains in honor of the Lord and gives thanks to God. [7]None of us lives to himself, and none of us dies to himself. [8]If we live, we live to the Lord, and if we die, we die to the Lord; so then, whether we live or whether we die, we are the Lord's. [9]For to this end Christ died and lived again, that he might be Lord both of the dead and of the living.

[10]Why do you pass judgment on your brother? Or you, why do you despise your brother? For we shall all stand before the judgment seat of God; [11]for it is written,

"As I live, says the Lord, every knee shall bow to me, and every tongue shall give praise to God."

[12]So each of us shall give account of himself to God.

The observance of fasting and of "holy" days is part of the religious history of the human race. Vegetarianism, for example, was known among both the Greeks and the Jews as well as among the early Christians. It was the motivation behind such practices that determined their religious value. Thus, if fasting was practiced in order to placate an angry divinity, this would have to be denounced as pagan and sinful. Paul realized that abstention from meat offered to pagan idols was not necessary because idols did not exist, but he also recognized that there were those who were concerned about such meat and he did not want to wound their weak consciences (1 Cor 8). In general the same concern is shown here.

The one anomaly that appears in this passage is that, while asking the Roman Christians not to pass judgment on their brothers (v.10), Paul does, in effect, judge them himself. It is true that he does not make a moral judgment on them in the sense of condemning them as he condemned the incestuous man in 1 Cor 5:1-5. And that is what he really asks them to avoid in v. 10. But his designation of those who abstain from meat as the "weak" is a judgment that the faith of those people is not of the caliber of his own. Indeed, it would seem, at least to us today, that the whole passage of

14:1 to 15:13 would strike the "weak" Christians as patronizing. This may be partly relieved by the possibility that he did not know any of the "weak" Christians at Rome personally. It would, of course, be altogether relieved if, as some hold, he was not intending a reference to a specific situation in Rome. At any rate, no commentator ever did accuse Paul of not being forthright, even when writing on the most delicate of matters!

Christians are to "welcome" the weak in faith, that is, receive them into their company as they would any others. Although the "weak" are probably that way because of a lack of sufficient catechesis, the Romans are not to welcome them in a contentious spirit, for the sake of "setting them right" (v.1). The vegetarian of v.2 is not the modern "health fan" who avoids meat because of dietary reasons; such a one could hardly be called "weak." Rather, it is the one who avoids foods because of religious reasons; such a one has a delicate conscience. No moral judgment should be made by either group on the other, since, as Christians, they have obviously been "welcomed" (the same Greek word as in v.1) by God (v.3). The "servant" (literally, a "domestic") of v.4 is the one "who eats" of v.3, who is said to be a member of God's household and so is not to be judged by the "weak." As such a servant, the "eater" is in God's hands, the same God who judges who it is who stands or falls and who upholds his own.

In almost every religion certain days are marked off for special purposes, such as fasting. These days were not universally observed in the same way by all Christians in the early church. The one criterion that Paul proposes for this variety of practice is religious conviction. As he says clearly in v.6, whatever is done should be done "for the Lord." Both the one who fasts and the one who eats give thanks at their meals. Living and dying to one's self (v.7) means doing so without a necessary reference to God. For Paul this is impossible. We live and die as the Lord's servants or property. Simply, "we are the Lord's." This lordship of Christ was attained through his salvific death and resurrection.

Through the latter especially was he freed of all restrictions to the full exercise of his lordship (cf. 1:4) and thus he really can be and is lord of both the dead and the living. Some suggest that vv. 7-9 may be part of an ancint baptismal hymn, similar to Eph 5:14. Paul does associate life and death with Christ with the sacrament of baptism in 6:3-11. The order expressed here, "the dead and the living," is unusual, but may be explained by the baptismal suggestion of death to sin and life with Christ.

The two questions of v.10 could be addressed to the "weak" who judge the "strong" and to the "strong" who despise the "weak." Both attitudes are meaningless in the face of both groups' appearance before a transcendent judgment seat which is both all-encompassing and ultimate. A Scripture quote based on Is 45:23 supports the universal lordship which demands a response, not of judgment on the other, but of adoration and praise of God.

RESPECTING THE OTHER'S CONSCIENCE. 14:13-23.

Thus far in this chapter Paul has been encouraging mutual respect. As we just saw, the "strong" are not to despise the "weak," nor are the "weak" to condemn the "strong" for being too liberal. Still, in the very designation of the one group as "weak," Paul had tipped his hand as to which he thought needed the more protection. He makes this clear now when he advises the "strong" to be sensitive to the tender consciences of the others and to respect their situation. What he says in effect is that holiness can at times depend on purely subjective principles.

13Then let us no more pass judgment on one another, but rather decide never to put a stumbling block or hindrance in the way of a brother. 14I know and am persuaded in the Lord Jesus that nothing is unclean in itself; but it is unclean for any one who thinks it unclean. [15]If your brother is being injured by what you eat, you are no longer walking in love. Do not let what you eat cause the ruin of one for whom Christ died. [16]So do not let your good be spoken of as evil. [17]For the kingdom of God is not food and drink but righteousness and peace and joy in the Holy Spirit; [18]he who thus serves Christ is acceptable to God and approved by men. [19]Let us then pursue what makes for peace and for mutual upbuilding. [20]Do not, for the sake of food, destroy the work of God. Everything is indeed clean, but it is wrong for any one to make others fall by what he eats; [21]it is right not to eat meat or drink wine or do anything that makes your brother stumble. [22]The faith that you have, keep between yourself and God; happy is he who has no reason to judge himself for what he approves. [23]But he who has doubts is condemned, if he eats, because he does not act from faith; for whatever does not proceed from faith is sin.

The first part of v. 13 summarizes what he has already said about not judging others. The word "judge" then serves as a catch-word (in the Greek) for the word "decide." So, instead of judging others we should judge not to harm them in any way. The "stumbling block" is probably an unintended barrier, while the "hindrance" (*skandalon*) suggests a deliberate trap. Both should be avoided. In order to show how such obstacles could result in the particular case of eating certain foods, he has first to enunciate the principle (v. 14). He is absolutely convinced "in the Lord Jesus that nothing is unclean in itself." This conviction could well rest on the strong statement made by Jesus in Mk 7:14-23 (cf. especially vv. 18-19). This was a radical departure from Jewish law with its insistence on "kosher" food and on various forms of ritual uncleanness. It is quite understandable if some Christians (the "weak" ones) had difficulty in accepting this and continued to abstain from certain foods. Paul is sensitive to this difficulty, so much so that he can say that something, even though not unclean in itself, is unclean for the one who thinks it is. It is this subjective element in moral decision making that dominates the passage.

In v.15 he addresses the "strong" directly. Love of the other must be the guiding principle, as he had already stressed (13:8-10). And love will cause no injury, or pain, or distress. In v.15b he puts it much more forcefully, "Do not destroy that one (the "brother") by your food . . ." The value of that "brother" is so great because Christ died for him. The destruction would come about by the "weak" brother being led to eat food that he was convinced he should not eat. Thus he would sin by acting contrary to his own conscience. Paul takes this seriously indeed. The "strong" Christian's liberty to eat anything at all (that is the meaning of "your good" in v.16) should be willingly sacrificed so that a privilege might not be falsely reviled by the "weak" as an abuse.

In vv.17 to 19 we have three positive statements on the question. Again, the apostle's seriousness is manifest in his seeing a relationship here to the kingdom of God. If that transcendent reality were somehow radically associated with what we eat and drink, then the "strong" Christian would have to ignore the "weak" one's situation and always live out the conviction that nothing is unclean in itself; the Christian must never distinguish between foods. But since the kingdom has to do radically with other realities, "righteousness and peace and joy in the Holy Spirit," the Christians' privilege with regard to food has to take second place Paul knows that these ideals have not yet been fully realized, but he also knows that if we do not strive for them in our relationships with others, the Christian enterprise might as well be abandoned. Striving for them is to serve Christ (v.18) and serving Christ in this way makes us "acceptable to God and approved by men." Behind that phrase stands the indissoluble two-fold command to love God and neighbor, which is involved in this whole discussion. That is why we should strive for peace and for whatever contributes to the common good (v.19). Paul was deeply concerned that the common good take precedence over individual satisfaction, as his whole treatment of the gifts of the Spirit in 1 Cor 12-14 brings out (cf. especially 12:7).

The "work of God" (v.20) in the context (cf. v.15b) would be the "weak" Christian, although some see it as the Christian community which would be disrupted by an untoward championing of one's rights. If it is "wrong" to make others fall by what is eaten, then it becomes "right" to abstain from whatever would bring that about. Thus, the unusual situation, evaluated now in the light of Christian love, makes wrong what would ordinarily be right and makes right what would ordinarily be at best a neutral value, that is, abstaining from food (vv.20-21). V.22 seems better understood addressed to the "strong," not to both groups. The conviction about one's liberty to eat anything at all should be maintained, above all in one's faith life with God. Such a person does not have to be concerned about what is acceptable for eating. But the "weak" Christian who eats while doubting that it is right acts contrary to conscience and so commits sin (v.23). Paul concludes the passage with a general principle that anything done contrary to one's faith life with God is a sin. It is a principle with which any religious person would agree.

AS CHRIST HAS DONE
15:1-13.

Paul's final remarks on this matter of conscience are contained in this passage. The thrust is positive, encouraging, prayerful. The obligations of Christians to their neighbors are highlighted by the example of Christ who was "the man for others." A prayer (v.13) is a fitting concluding statement on the whole matter.

> **15** We who are strong ought to bear with the failings of the weak, and not to please ourselves; ²let each of us please his neighbor for his good, to edify him. ³For Christ

did not please himself; but, as it is written, "The reproaches of those who reproached thee fell on me." [4]For whatever was written in former days was written for our instruction, that by steadfastness and by the encouragement of the scriptures we might have hope. [5]May the God of steadfastness and encouragement grant you to live in such harmony with one another, in accord with Christ Jesus, [6]that together you may with one voice glorify the God and Father of our Lord Jesus Christ.

[7]Welcome one another, therefore, as Christ has welcomed you, for the glory of God. [8]For I tell you that Christ became a servant to the circumcised to show God's truthfulness, in order to confirm the promises given to the patriarchs, [9]and in order that the Gentiles might glorify God for his mercy. As it is written,

"Therefore I will praise thee among the Gentiles,
and sing to thy name";
[10]and again it is said,
"Rejoice, O Gentiles, with his people";
[11]and again,
"Praise the Lord, all Gentiles,
and let all the peoples praise him";
[12]and further Isaiah says,
"The root of Jesse shall come,
he who rises to rule the Gentiles;
in him shall the Gentiles hope."
[13]May the God of hope fill you with all joy and peace in believing, so that by the power of the Holy Spirit you may abound in hope.

For the first time the "strong" are explicitly mentioned, though they were addressed already in 14:13. But it is clear that their strength or power is mentioned by Paul not as something to be boasted about but as something to use for others, in this case for "the weak" whose failings they are to bear. To "bear" here means not simply to tolerate but to accept as a burden for which one takes responsibility (cf. Lk

14:27). In the case under discussion it can be done in several ways: by sacrificing one's own freedom when necessary (as already stated in 14:15-21), by encouraging the "weak" in their faith, even by trying sensitively to open them up to a broader vision. The principle, once again, is pleasing others rather than just uplifting or giving good example to others; it suggests positive support and instruction.

The selflessness of Christ is introduced in v.3. The Scripture reference is to Ps 69:9 where the psalmist is saying that his zeal for the Lord's house had somehow caused fellow-Israelites to reproach him. Paul applies this to Christ. God's enemies become his enemies and he suffers their reproaches. Paul quotes the passage as though it had been originally intended as referring to Christ. But that is how the early Church read the Old Testament, that is, as saying something to their own situation as followers of Christ. The Word of God was always a living, active Word concerned with the present. Paul says this effectively in v.4. Behind this lies the conviction of a profound unity in God's self-revelation. Nothing that God reveals of himself stands isolated or just for the moment. Especially important for Christians in that instruction from "former days" are words of "steadfastness" and "encouragement." It might be that the first is intended especially for the "strong" and the second for the "weak." More likely is it that both are needed by all in order to overcome divisions and to live in harmony (v.5). The "harmony" doesn't necessarily mean agreement in all things, especially in the matter under discussion. But they would at least be accepting of one another to such an extent that they would be able "with one voice" to "glorify the God and Father of our Lord Jesus Christ" (v.6). Only a united Church can most effectively honor the one God.

Again, in v.7, the example of Christ is cited as a motivation for the Romans' acceptance or welcome of one another. Christ welcomed them fully by not making any distinctions between Jew and Gentile. They should welcome one another by not making any distinction between the "strong" and "weak" as far as acceptance is concerned. That would seem to be behind Paul's thought in v.7 in view of his constant emphasis in his letters on Christ's saving action for all, and in view of the verses that follow. In v.8 he affirms God's "truthfulness" in that Christ became a Jew ("a servant to the circumcised"), thereby fulfilling his promises of a Messiah to the forefathers. (The promise of a Messiah was in reality much later than the patriarchs, but Paul, together with the early Christians generally, would see that promise already contained implicitly in the more general promises made to Abraham, Isaac and Jacob.) What was a show of God's truthfulness to the Jewish people became a show of his mercy to the Gentiles (v.9). This was because it was out of unmotivated love that the pagans were granted access to the Christian faith. It is this mercy to the Gentiles that is emphasized by the quotations from Ps 18:49, Dt 32:43, Ps 17:1, and Is 11:10. The rather free renderings of these passages is typical of many contained in what are thought to be lists of "testimonies" used by the early Church for apologetic purposes.

A question that is raised in the context of the "Jew and Gentile" distinction is whether Paul was identifying them, implicitly, with the two groups that have been the subject of discussion. Some hold that the Jewish Christians would be more likely to be identified with the "weak," since their Jewish past would have provided the springboard for holding on to special days of fast or to abstention from certain foods. The converts from paganism would not have developed such scruples. It is doubtful, however, that Paul would have intended such an identification, especially since his reference to Jews and Gentiles can be explained by his constant and almost overwhelming consciousness of God's favor to both these groups manifested in different ways.

The concluding prayer is rich with biblical themes and expresses Paul's deep concern that the Christian community be not shattered by divisions. His experience of this at Corinth no doubt lay heavily upon him and helps to explain his emphasis in this prayer both on peace and on hope. Peace, in the biblical sense, meant a fulness of God's blessings manifested in living relationships. When it is had, it is understandably accompanied by joy. That Paul sees this peace as God-given is clear from his addition of the phrase "in believing." It is had, in other words, in the act of surrendering acceptance of the self-revealing God. Hope is a virtue that looks to the future with confidence and optimism. This, too, is God-given as Paul indicates by attributing it to "the power of the Holy Spirit." One is immediately reminded of his impressive statements on the role of the Spirit in the Christian's life in c. 8. Thus, the prayer fittingly concludes the discussion of what Paul considered a serious problem.

CONCLUDING PERSONAL REMARKS
15:14-33

The introduction to the letter (1:1-15) had consisted of personal remarks by Paul concerning his mission and his attitude toward the Roman Church. These same kinds of remarks make up this conclusion. There are two principal sections in this passage. The first (15:14-21) takes up what he has done as a missionary. The second (15:22-33) takes up what he plans to do in the future.

CHRIST'S PRIESTLY MISSIONARY.
15:14-21.

Using his relationship to the Romans as a springboard, Paul offers a careful and thoughtful explanation of his apostolate. There are some excellent theological insights into ministry here.

> [14]I myself am satisfied about you, my brethren, that you yourselves are full of goodness, filled with all knowledge, and able to instruct one another. [15]But on some points I have written to you very boldly by way of reminder, because of the grace given me by God [16]to be a minister of Christ Jesus to the Gentiles in the priestly service of the gospel of God, so that the offering of the Gentiles may be acceptable, sanctified by the Holy Spirit. [17]In Christ Jesus, then, I have reason to be proud of my work for

God. [18]For I will not venture to speak of anything except what Christ has wrought through me to win obedience from the Gentiles, by word and deed, [19]by the power of signs and wonders, by the power of the Holy Spirit, so that from Jerusalem and as far round as Illyricum I have fully preached the gospel of Christ, [20]thus making it my ambition to preach the gospel, not where Christ has already been named, lest I build on another man's foundation, [21]but as it is written,

"They shall see who have never been told of him,

and they shall understand who have never heard of him."

Paul begins a most gracious statement about the Roman Christians. If it were someone other than Paul, it could be considered obsequious. But that is not Paul's way. "Goodness" and "knowledge" can assure both orthopraxis (correct action) and orthodoxy (correct doctrine). Because of that they are quite capable of providing the necessary catechesis for the community. Some have found this v.14 difficult to believe in the light of what he had written in the preceding chapters. But those ethical exhortations need not be understood as reflecting serious problems in the Christian community. It is just that, when Paul speaks on any subject, he speaks boldly and forthrightly, reflecting potential problems, not necessarily real ones. And he himself says (v.15) that his bold remarks were intended as a reminder of what they had already been taught.

What is more, the remarks were sparked by the apostle's strong sense of vocation and mission to the Gentiles (vv. 15b-16). That kind of gift demands responsible action and Paul was not one to shirk it. The rich liturgical language of v.16 reveals the religious depths of Paul's conviction about his ministry. He is a *leitourgos*, that is, a cultic official of Jesus Christ for the Gentiles. He serves the gospel as a priest (*hierourgeō*, used only here in the New

Testament, from the word meaning "holy"). In other words, he considers preaching a cultic or liturgical rite. Finally, he offers up to God the Gentiles who have been made holy or consecrated by the Holy Spirit and so are acceptable. In his role, then, as a cultic or priestly missionary, he has the obligation to speak boldly. So strongly does he perceive this that he says something that is close to heresy for him otherwise. In v.17 he writes, literally, "I have therefore boasting in Christ Jesus concerning the things pertaining to God." The boasting does involve himself obviously, but it is "in Christ Jesus," which means that Jesus is the real source of any good in him.

This last thought is spelled out more clearly in vv.18-19. Any words of his, and especially any boasting, are directed only to what Christ has done through him. Paul has made it clear elsewhere that it is Christ who lives in him (Gal 2:20) and who makes it possible for him to do all things (Phil 4:13). He lists the more important means used to achieve this "obedience from the Gentiles." "Word and deed" are a kind of summary of Jesus' own mission (cf. Mt 4:23) and refer to his teaching, preaching and healing. The Acts of the Apostles shows abundantly that the apostles, including Paul, shared that ministry. "Signs and wonders" are two words frequently used together, especially in Acts, to indicate miraculous feats. The "power of the Holy Spirit" is not properly a means like the others. For Paul, especially in the light of c.8, the Spirit has to be considered the originating principle making all other means possible. In that power Paul has made the "circle of the nations." Illyricum, or Dalmatia, was a name for the coastland on the eastern side of the Adriatic Sea, to the north of Greece. Through his preaching Paul had founded Christian communities throughout the lands embraced by Illyricum and Jerusalem (v.19). Just how much apostolic activity he exercised in the two frontiers is not clear.

In doing this Paul had the basic rule to preach only among the non-Christians (v.20). He did not want to "build on another man's foundation," not out of a fear of competition, but out of a sense of urgency in getting the gospel "started" like a fire in as many places as possible. He would not go "where Christ has already been named." The last phrase can mean where Christ was invoked, as in prayer, or simply where he was known. He sees this practice as a fulfillment of Is 52:15, quoted from the Greek translation. It is part of the famous "Suffering Servant" poem so often applied to Christ in the New Testament.

FUTURE PLANS.
15:22-33.

Despite all that he has accomplished in Christ, Paul still has great ambitions for the future. He wants to take a special collection to the poor of Jerusalem, then go on to Rome, but only for a visit. He wants to go on from there to Spain, apparently still virgin territory as far as Christianity is concerned.

> [22]This is the reason why I have so often been hindered from coming to you. [23]But now, since I no longer have any room for work in these regions, and since I have longed for many years to come to you, [24]I hope to see you in passing as I go to Spain, and to be sped on my journey there by you, once I have enjoyed your company for a little. [25]At present, however, I am going to Jerusalem with aid for the saints. [26]For Macedonia and Achaia have been pleased to make some contribution for the poor among the saints at Jerusalem; [27]they were pleased to do it, and indeed they are in debt to them, for if the Gentiles have come to share in their spiritual blessings, they ought also to be of service to them in material blessings. [28]When therefore I have completed this, and have delivered to them what has been raised, I shall go on by way of you to Spain; [29]and I know that when I come to you I shall come in the fulness of the blessing of Christ.

³⁰I appeal to you brethren, by our Lord Jesus Christ and by the love of the Spirit, to strive together with me in your prayers to God on my behalf, ³¹that I may be delivered from the unbelievers in Judea, and that my service for Jerusalem may be acceptable to the saints, ³²so that by God's will I may come to you with joy and be refreshed in your company. ³³The God of peace be with you all. Amen.

In 1:10 Paul had suggested that he wanted to come to Rome for some time. In v.20 he said that the reason he had not come was his concern for the non-evangelized places. Now he feels that he has substantially fulfilled his goal, though he would be the first to admit that there were still many communities that had not heard of the gospel. What could be said was that a spark had been ignited that would spread by the very power of the gospel. Thus he hoped now to fufill his desire to visit the Roman Church. In keeping with his principle (v.20), this would not be an evangelizing project, but only a visit on his way to a new mission in Spain (v.24). He even hoped that the Roman Christians would support his new mission in some way by "speeding him on his journey." There is some very early evidence that he did in fact reach Spain, but it is inconclusive. Most scholars think that he was put to death in Rome after the house arrest mentioned in Acts 28:30-31.

Before coming to Rome, he must complete a self-imposed assignment, taking a gift of money to the church at Jerusalem (vv.25-28). This gift from the Gentile communities was a great concern of Paul's (cf. 1 Cor 16:1-4; 2 Cor 8-9). It was not just a gesture of relief for the poor. It was to symbolize the unity of the Gentile Christians with the Jewish Christian mother-church in Jerusalem. Paul was most sensitive to the need for this unity precisely because of his experience of the reservations that the Jewish Christians had about his work among the Gentiles. Paul's own sincerity in this matter is clear from his wanting to tell the Romans that the Gentile communities *owed* this collection to the Jerusalem community because it was from the latter, the first Christian community, that the gospel itself had originated. Now it was only this task that had to be completed before he could proceed to Rome and Spain. In v.28 he says literally that "when I have sealed to them this fruit," he would go on to Rome. This refers to a process of authenticating a produce at the time of delivery. This helps us to understand why Paul felt he had to discharge this duty personally. He wanted to put his own "seal" on the gift. Once that is done, he is confident he can come bearing Christ's blessings. This is one more exercise of his priestly ministry (cf. v.16).

In the final verses Paul's anxiety is more sharply exposed. He begs the Romans to pray for him with regard to the plans he has outlined (v.30). He is obviously concerned about the outcome of his visit to Jerusalem. The "unbelievers in Judea" understandably considered him an apostate who was disrupting the Jewish communities by his apostolate (v.31). They could (and would) deal harshly with him when he came to Jerusalem. He also wanted the Romans to pray that the Jewish Christians would receive the collection graciously and in the spirit of unity in which it was given. The evidence on this point does not seem too favorable (cf. Acts 21:17-26). Finally, he asked that they would pray for a joyful and refreshing visit with them (v.32). This, too, was to be denied him, as he came to Rome a prisoner (Acts 28:16). He concludes this letter, as he had opened it (1:7), with a prayer for God's peace for them.

A CONCLUSION
16:1-27

We have deliberately used the ambiguous "a conclusion" as the heading for this section since it is questioned whether it is the original conclusion to our present letters. Paul mentions by name over twenty individuals known to him, though he had never been to Rome. Also, at least two of them, Prisca and Aquila, had fled Rome because of an edict of Claudius against the Jews (Acts 18:2). And Epaenetus (v.5) is said to be "the first convert in Asia." The strong words in vv.17-18, moreover, do not seem to fit the tone of the rest of the letter. For these and other reasons a number of scholars think this to be the conclusion of another letter, perhaps a copy of this one (but without the mention of "Rome" in 1:7,15), originally sent to Ephesus. Other scholars find an adequate explanation for these inconsistencies and hold for its present position. We will make our comments on the basis of the latter position, aware that there is no absolute certainty in the matter. In any case, no doctrinal issues would be involved.

PAUL'S PERSONAL COMMENDATION
AND GREETINGS.
16:1-16.

He first commends Phoebe to their favor and then greets all those Christians known to him.

> **16** I commend to you our sister Phoebe, a deaconess of the church of Cenchreae, ²that you may receive her

in the Lord as befits the saints, and help her in whatever she may require from you, for she has been a helper of many and of myself as well.

[3]Greet Prisca and Aquila, my fellow workers in Christ Jesus, [4]who risked their necks for my life, to whom not only I but also all the churches of the Gentiles give thanks; [5]greet also the church in their house. Greet my beloved Epaenetus, who was the first convert in Asia for Christ. [6]Greet Mary, who has worked hard among you. [7]Greet Andronicus and Junias, my kinsmen and my fellow prisoners; they are men of note among the apostles, and they were in Christ before me. [8]Greet Ampliatus, my beloved in the Lord. [9]Greet Urbanus, our fellow worker in Christ, and my beloved Stachys. [10]Greet Apelles, who is approved in Christ. Greet those who belong to the family of Aristobulus. [11]Greet my kinsman Herodion. Greet those in the Lord who belong to the family of Narcissus. [12]Greet those workers in the Lord, Tryphaena and Tryphosa. Greet the beloved Persis, who has worked hard in the Lord. [13]Greet Rufus, eminent in the Lord, also his mother and mine. [14]Greet Asyncritus, Phlegon, Hermes, Patrobas, Hermas, and the brethren who are with them. [15]Greet Philologus, Julia, Nereus and his sister, and Olympas, and all the saints who are with them. [16]Greet one another with a holy kiss. All the churches of Christ greet you.

Phoebe, a Christian woman who had been a "helper" (*prostatis*, perhaps "protectress" or "patroness") of many besides Paul, is otherwise unknown to us. She is called a *diakonos* which, despite its masculine form, can properly be translated "deaconess." It is used in a general sense for one who serves (v.g., 2 Cor 11:23) or in a more technical sense of one who has an ecclesiastical office (1 Tim 3:8). The context here suggests the latter, which brings up the much debated question of an order of "deaconnesses" in the early church. Cenchreae was a port city about seven miles

from Corinth, Paul's place of residence at the time. Like
so many others (nine) in this section who are greeted or in
some way characterized as "in the Lord" or "in Christ,"
Phoebe is to be received "in the Lord." That is the way
Christians ("the saints") act.

Paul calls Epaenetus (v.5) his "first convert in Asia." The
Greek literally has the "first fruits of Asia" for Christ. In
using that word he probably sees this Christian as not only
the first but also as representative of all the other converts in
this Roman province which embraced the western part of
modern Turkey. The "Mary" of v.6 is not known. Andronicus and Junias (v.7) were among the earliest Jewish converts to Christianity (before Paul). They were imprisoned
with him (where is unknown) and, like him, are called
apostles, a term obviously used for others than the "Twelve."
Some suggest that Junias is the wife of Andronicus, which,
if true, would have some bearing on the role of women in
the early church hierarchy. (In that case the RSV translation
of the rest of the verse would have to be slightly changed:
"kinsmen," "fellow," "men.")

None of those named in vv.8-15 is known with certitude.
Most of the names have been found in Roman inscriptions,
which proves nothing except that they were common names.
Some have argued that Mark, in his Gospel, mentions Rufus
as the son of Simon of Cyrene (15:21) because he was well
known to the Roman church. If that is true, then the identification with the Rufus of v.13 becomes a possibility. A
striking feature of the list is that Paul seems to know most
of them personally, at times mentioning some special
characteristic (Ampliatus, Urbanus, Apelles, Herodion,
Persis, Rufus). If the chapter belongs in its present place,
then all these would have migrated to Rome from some
other place where Paul had come into contact with them.
The manner in which Paul exhorts them to exchange "a
holy kiss" (a ritual embrace) here (v.16) and elsewhere
(1 Cor 16:20; 2 Cor 13:12; 1 Thess 5:26) is a sufficient
indication that it was a common custom among the early
Christians.

EXPRESSION OF CONCERN; GREETINGS FROM PAUL'S CO-WORKERS. 16:17-23.

An unexpected note of concern interrupts Paul's personal greetings, but it is quickly followed by greetings from other Christians in Corinth.

> [17]I appeal to you, brethren, to take note of those who create dissensions and difficulties, in opposition to the doctrine which you have been taught; avoid them. [18]For such persons do not serve our Lord Christ, but their own appetites, and by fair and flattering words they deceive the hearts of the simple-minded. [19]For while your obedience is known to all, so that I rejoice over you, I would have you wise as to what is good and guileless as to what is evil; [20]then the God of peace will soon crush Satan under your feet. The grace of our Lord Jesus Christ be with you.
>
> [21]Timothy, my fellow worker, greets you; so do Lucius and Jason and Sosipater, my kinsmen.
>
> [22]I Tertius, the writer of this letter, greet you in the Lord.
>
> [23]Gaius, who is host to me and to the whole church, greets you. Erastus, the city treasurer, and our brother Quartus, greet you.

Several times in his letters Paul indicates that he writes the concluding section in his own hand (cf. 2 Thess 3:17; 1 Cor 16:21; Col 4:18). He does the same in Gal 6:11-18, but there he expands his thought greatly, repeating the warning expressed earlier in his "angry letter." So the expansion here in Romans is not without precedent, although the warning is not as in place here as it is in Galatians. It would be more in place in a letter to the Church at Ephesus, where Paul had had so much experience.

In any case the readers are warned to avoid those who would cause dissensions or occasions for apostasy. In v. 18 he says they serve "their own appetites." The word literally is "belly," a word he uses also in Phil 3:19 in the same sense. It is a form of self-serving that may express itself in undue concern for kosher foods, or, more likely here, in illicit pleasures. Some would associate these persons with Gnostics who held that, as long as they had received the divine "knowledge" (*gnōsis* in Greek), they could indulge their appetites as they wished. The Romans' widely acclaimed "obedience" (i.e., of faith) is all the greater reason for exercising good judgment in assessing the good and for retaining their innocence of evil (v. 19). In Jewish literature the serpent that occasioned the first sin is identified as Satan or the devil (cf. Wis 2:24). When Paul says that God will crush Satan "under your feet," he is probably intending an allusion to the serpent of Gen 3:15. It is precisely as the God "of peace" that he will restore the wholeness of being brought about by the symbolic agent of disorder and division. The blessing of v.20b is omitted in some manuscripts but is common with Paul (1 Cor 16:23; 2 Cor 13:14; Gal 6:18).

Paul then adds the greetings of those close to him at Corinth (vv.21-23). The following names are found elsewhere in the New Testament: Timothy (Acts 16:1-3), Lucius (Acts 13:1), Jason (Acts 17:5-9), Sosipater (Acts 20:4, but as Sopater), Gaius (1 Cor 1:14). Of these Timothy alone can be certainly identified. Tertius, Paul's secretary, who has taken over the writing again, adds his greetings (v.22). The presence of a public official, Erastus, among the highly respected Christians at Corinth shows that Christianity had an appeal not only to the lower classes. V.24, a repetition of v.20b, is omitted in the better manuscripts. (RSV has it in a footnote.)

GLORY TO GOD.
16:25-27.

This concluding doxology is made up of one complex sentence in the Greek. Because Paul does not usually conclude his letters with such hymns of praise, because "the revelation of the mystery" is not mentioned elsewhere in Romans, and because the style and vocabulary are not readily recognized as Pauline, many scholars think this passage was added later by a non-Pauline author.

> 25Now to him who is able to strengthen you according to my gospel and the preaching of Jesus Christ, according to the revelation of the mystery which was kept secret for long ages 26but is now disclosed and through the prophetic writings is made known to all nations, according to the command of the eternal God, to bring about the obedience of faith—27to the only wise God be glory for evermore through Jesus Christ! Amen.

There are three elements in this doxology: what God has done or is doing for Christians, how he has done it, and the Christian response. What God does is to strengthen Christians in their faith (v.25) and to bring pagans to the "obedience of faith" (v.26c). God does this through Paul's own gospel, which does not mean, of course, the good news about him, but about Jesus Christ. The "preaching of Jesus Christ" is to be taken as an objective genitive: Jesus Christ is the object of (Paul's) preaching. This gospel is not something that burst forth into a world totally unprepared for it. The "mystery," or plan, was really announced by the prophets long ago, but it was not understood until "now," the eschatological "now" of end-time fulfillment. The prophetic writings are now understood in their fulness and can be proclaimed to the world. The "command of the eternal God" emphasizes both the divine initiative, a favorite Pauline theme, and the continuity of the plan ("the *eternal* God"). The Christian response to all this is the giving of glory to God always through Jesus Christ. This is the proper climax of the hymn (cf. Phil 2:11) and is a fitting climax of the message of the entire letter. Giving glory to God is what Christians do *as Christians* because of what God has done through his Son.

Select Bibliography

C.K. Barrett, *A Commentary on the Epistle to the Romans (Harper's New Testament Commentaries)*, Harper, New York, 1957.
> Author's translation of the Greek with responsible commentary. Among the better shorter studies.

E. Best, *The Letter of Paul to the Romans (The Cambridge Bible Commentary on the New English Bible)*, Cambridge, 1967.
> A solid, balanced exegesis of the letter based on the provocative version of the NEB.

C.H. Dodd, *The Epistle of Paul to the Romans*, Collins, London, 1959.
> An older (first published in 1932) commentary that has enduring value. Excellent developments of select passages.

J.A. Fitzmyer, *The Letter to the Romans (Jerome Biblical Commentary)*, Prentice-Hall, Englewood Cliffs, 1968.
> A concise commentary with superb control of all the technical data.

J. Knox, *The Epistle to the Romans (The Interpreter's Bible)*, Abingdon-Cokesbury, Nashville, 1954.
> Fine command of all the issues involved. Thorough.

F.J. Leenhardt, *The Epistle to the Romans*, World Publishing Co., Cleveland, 1961.
> A translation from the French. A thorough, scholarly discussion of the letter.

T.W. Manson, *Romans (Peake's Commentary on the Bible)*, Nelson, London, 1962.
> A concise, scholarly exegesis.

K.H. Schelkle, *The Epistle to the Romans*, Herder and Herder, New York, 1964.
> A translation from the German. Meditative and scholarly reflections on the letter, frequently indicating contemporary relevance.

J.D. Smart, *Doorway to a New Age*, Westminster, Philadelphia, 1972.

A fine study of the letter in the form of a running commentary, not verse by verse, with many contemporary applications.

V. Taylor, *The Epistle to the Romans (Epworth Preacher's Commentaries)*, Epworth Press, London, 1955.

A series of concise, at times brilliant, notes on the individual verses.

K.P. Donfried (ed.), *The Romans Debate*, Augsburg, Minneapolis, 1977.

Ten essays by European and American scholars on special questions concerning the letter. Excellent background material.